By the same author

How to Cheat at Chess

The Penguin Book of Chess Openings

Soft Pawn

The Ultimate Irrelevant Encyclopedia

The Kings of Chess

Chess – The Making of the Musical

The Drunken Goldfish and Other Irrelevant Scientific Research

How was it for you, Professor?

The Guinness Book of Chess Grandmasters

Teach Yourself Chess

Teach Yourself Better Chess

The Book of Numbers: The Ultimate Compendium

of Facts About Figures

Mr Hartston's Most Excellent Encyclopedia of Useless Information

Forgotten Treasures: A Collection of Well-Loved Poetry (Vols 1, 2 and 3)

The Things That Nobody Knows

Even More Things That Nobody Knows

The Bumper Book of Things That Nobody Knows

Sloths

William
HARTSTON
A
BRIEF
HISTORY
OF PUZZLES

BAFFLING BRAINTEASERS
from the
SPHINX TO SUDOKU

Atlantic Books
London

First published in hardback in Great Britain in 2019
by Atlantic Books, an imprint of Atlantic Books Ltd.

1 2 3 4 5 6 7 8 9

A CIP catalogue record for this book is available
from the British Library.

Hardback ISBN: 978-1-78649-426-9
E-book ISBN: 978-1-78649-428-3

Designed by carrdesignstudio.com
Illustrations by Nathan Burton
Printed in Italy by ⬛ Grafica Veneta

Atlantic Books
An Imprint of Atlantic Books Ltd
Ormond House
26–27 Boswell Street
London
WC1N 3JZ

CONTENTS

ACKNOWLEDGEMENTS

From my childhood to my years as a chess player and mathematician and beyond, I have always held a fascination for the challenge of puzzles and I must express great gratitude to the many people who have fuelled this passion. First came writers such as Lewis Carroll, Henry Dudeney and Sam Loyd, whose books and articles awoke my interest in the recreational side of thinking. More recently, I have been inspired, amused and infuriated by modern puzzlers such as Martin Gardner, Raymond Smullyan, Chris Maslanka, David Bodycombe, Alex Bellos and Prof. David Singmaster, all of whom have unwittingly given me ideas for this book. These, incidentally, are among the best names to look out for if you're looking for the most tantalizing books of puzzles. I am happy to count several of these among my friends and they are the most mentally stimulating company anyone could wish for.

I must also thank all those who have put up with my endless puzzling while I have been collecting puzzles for this book, and my *Gogglebox* companion Josef Kollar who has been as willing to tantalize me with puzzles as I am with him.

Finally, I should like to thank Cambridge psychology professors Trevor Robbins and Barbara Sahakian for treating me to a splendid breakfast during which they explained how puzzles, quite apart from being fun, may actually be good for you.

'Evolution has developed the brain's ability to solve puzzles, and at the same time has produced in our brain a pleasure of solving problems.'

Martin Gardner, recreational mathematics writer, interviewed in the *New York Times*, 19 October 2009

PRIMEVAL PUZZLE
PRELUDE

❓ PUZZLE 1

An infuriating fellow took 120 puzzles to try out on some schoolchildren, which, by a remarkable coincidence, is the number of puzzles for you to solve in this book. The first-year children solved some of these, so he gave the second year a larger number of different puzzles, which they also solved. The third year were given even more, as were the fourth year and the fifth year. Each time, the number of puzzles went up by the same amount and at the end he had used up all his puzzles. The total number given to the three highest years was exactly seven times the number given to the first two years. How many puzzles were given to each year?

The answer to Puzzle 1, and the other 119 numbered puzzles in this book, can be found in the Solutions section at the end of this book.

The language used in Puzzle 1 is different and the scenario modernized, but the puzzle is basically problem number 40 in the Rhind Papyrus, a remarkable ancient Egyptian mathematical manuscript that has a good claim on being the oldest puzzle book. Compiled by a scribe called Ahmes or Ahmose around 1550 BC, but known to have borrowed items from works two or three centuries older, it was bought by the Scottish antiquarian Alexander Henry Rhind in Luxor in 1858 and has been kept in the British Museum since 1865.

Containing 91 mathematical problems, divided into arithmetic, geometry and miscellaneous, the papyrus is essentially a mathematics textbook written in a teasing manner to encourage readers to develop the necessary techniques themselves. A modern reader, of course, would find it easy to solve the puzzle given above by using a little algebra, but the ancient Egyptians had to improvise other methods. The first algebra treatise was written around AD 830 by the medieval Persian mathematician, Muhammad ibn Mūsā al-Khwārizmī. He gave his treatise a long name in Arabic, which included the word *al-ğabr*, meaning 'the reunion of broken parts', and puzzlers and mathematicians have called his method 'algebra' ever since.

Long before Ahmes set brush to papyrus in Luxor, however, that same city, under its ancient name of Thebes, was the setting for a supposedly much older puzzle of Greek myth. According to the ancients, the city lived in terror of the Sphinx, a ferocious creature with the head of a woman and the body of a lion – in some versions also the wings of an eagle and the tail of a serpent – who had been sent by the gods to punish the Thebans for ancient crimes. The Sphinx was said to kill people who wished to enter Thebes by strangulation (incidentally, the connection between the Sphinx and our similarly named 'sphincter' muscles is that both words are derived from a Greek verb meaning to squeeze or strangle) – but, to give her victims a chance, she would first pose them a riddle. If they could not solve it, they were killed.

Nobody ever solved the riddle until Oedipus came along. The riddle the Sphinx asked Oedipus was this: 'What goes in the morning upon four feet, in the afternoon upon two feet, and in the evening on three feet?' Oedipus gave the answer 'Man', who crawls on all fours in the morning of his life, walks on two legs in the afternoon of his life, and needs a third leg in the form of a walking stick to get around in the evening of his old age. The Sphinx was so annoyed that Oedipus had solved the riddle that she threw herself to her death from a clifftop and Thebes was saved from her terror.

The idea of a hero being prepared to risk his life on his ability to solve riddles has been very powerful throughout history. One modern example comes in J. R. R. Tolkien's *The Hobbit*, where Bilbo Baggins and Gollum pose each other riddles. One of Bilbo's riddles is clearly inspired by the myth of the Sphinx: 'No-legs lay on one-leg, two-legs sat near on three-legs, four-legs got some.'

The explanation, rather more convoluted than Oedipus' answer, is that it refers to a fish (no legs) lying on a pedestal table (one leg), at which a man (two legs) is sitting on a three-legged stool and a cat (four legs) gets the scraps.

Another potentially fatal riddle format is seen in the plot of Puccini's opera *Turandot*, where the icy princess of the title sets her suitors three riddles in a thoroughly sadistic *Who Wants To Marry A Princess?* game show format: if they want to wed her, they must answer three riddles; if they get them wrong, their heads are lopped off.

Puccini got the plot from a work by Friedrich Schiller, which was itself an adaptation of a play by the eighteenth-century Italian dramatist and count, Carlo Gozzi. But Gozzi took the story from a work by the twelfth-century Persian poet Nizami Ganjavi, which comprises seven stories, one for each day of the week. Tuesday's tale was about a cold Russian princess called Turan-Dokht. Puccini's operatic version moves the story to China, where Prince Calaf falls in love at first sight with the imperious princess Turandot and submits himself to her riddles.

The first riddle is this: 'In the gloomy night, an iridescent phantom flies. It spreads its wings and rises over infinite, black humanity. Everyone invokes it, everyone implores it! But the phantom disappears at dawn to be reborn in the heart.'

Calaf gives the answer 'Hope', which is deemed correct, although I am not convinced it completely satisfies the specifications in Turandot's riddle.

The second riddle is: 'It flickers like flame, but is not flame! Sometimes it rages. It is feverish, impetuous, burning, but idleness changes it to languor. If you are lost or defeated, it turns cold. If you dream of winning, it bursts into flame. It has a faint voice, but you listen; it gleams as bright as the sunset!'

Calaf's answer is 'Blood', which sets him up for the final question: 'Ice that sets you on fire, and through your fire becomes more frosty! Immaculate but dark, if it sets you free, you become a slave! If you become a slave, it makes you king.'

That's an easy one, and Calaf sees that the answer is Turandot herself.

In ancient times, however, puzzles did not appear only in stories but seem to have been a part of everyday life. Drawings of labyrinths in ancient Greece and Egypt have been dated to before 2000 BC; the ancient Romans had puzzle locks with secret levers; the ancient Chinese from as early as the third century had chains of puzzle rings designed to challenge people to untangle them. The existence of such puzzles in many cultures suggests that people have always liked to tease each other by setting them problems.

The earliest puzzles of all took the form of riddles, mechanical devices and teasing tricks, and their appeal has lasted throughout the ages. The problems that involve pure thinking may have begun with maths lessons in ancient Egypt, but they have undergone a gentle transition to become something less didactic and more fun – and frustrating! And that transition is the subject of our first proper chapter on puzzles.

'The ingenious study of making and solving puzzles is a science undoubtedly of most necessary acquirement, and deserves to make a part in the meditation of both sexes.'

Sir Thomas Fitzosborne, pseudonym
of William Melmoth (1710–1799)

MEDIEVAL MATHS, MYSTERIES AND MERRIMENT

PUZZLES MAY HAVE begun in ancient times with riddles and teasing ways to introduce amusement into maths teaching but it took many more centuries before puzzles for puzzlement's sake alone became acceptable.

Remarkably, the earliest known collection of something similar to modern recreational puzzles dates back more than 1,200 years. It was probably assembled by Alcuin of York (*c*.735–804), a highly influential scholar and reformer of the early Christian church who acted as an adviser to the court of Charlemagne.

I say 'probably' because there is no definite evidence that the puzzles associated with Alcuin were actually composed or even just collected by him – although the puzzles were discovered at Charlemagne's court and one of Alcuin's letters to Charlemagne refers to 'subtle figures of arithmetic, for pleasure', which he says are included in the correspondence. Several copies of these *Propositiones ad acuendos iuvenes* (Propositions to Sharpen the Young) have been found, containing either 53 or 56 problems, presumably depending on which scribe copied the original manuscript. Several of the problems have also been found to date from even earlier times, which supports the view that Alcuin, or whoever assembled the manuscript in the first place, was essentially a collector of puzzles rather than their originator. They may have been intended, in Alcuin's words, as teaching devices to stimulate young minds, but the tone is impressively playful. Here are three of them, for which the solutions may be found at the end of this book.

? PUZZLE 2

A man and woman, each the weight of a cartload, with two children who together weigh as much as a cartload, have to cross a river. They find a boat but it can only take one cartload. Make the transfer if you can, without sinking the boat.

? PUZZLE 3

A man had to take a wolf, a goat and a bunch of cabbages across a river. The only boat he could find could only take two of them at a time. But he had been ordered to transfer all of these to the other side in good condition.

How could this be done without leaving the wolf alone with the goat (as he might eat it), or the goat alone with the cabbages (as it might eat them)?

❓ PUZZLE 4

A certain boy addressed his father, saying, 'Hello, father!' His father answered, 'Hello, my son. May you live to twice your present age and then at that time three times the age you will then be. If I gave you one of my years to add to this, then you will live to be 100 years old.' How old was the boy at the time?

Alcuin's river-crossing problems remain popular today, and several more convoluted versions have been concocted, often featuring cannibals and missionaries (who cannot be left with the former outnumbering the latter) or men and women (where no man can be left alone with another man's wife) or criminals who cannot be left without a police escort. Here is a typically complex modern example from a source in China.

❓ PUZZLE 5

A man, a woman, two boys, two girls, a policeman and a crook need to cross a river but the boat will only hold two people. The children cannot row the boat; the man cannot be in the presence of a girl if the woman is not present, and the woman cannot be left with a boy unless the man is there. The crook cannot be alone with any of the family without the policeman. All you have to do is get them all across the river.

We shall meet a final river-crossing puzzle on page 42.

After Alcuin's contributions in the eighth century, the world of puzzles seems to have stagnated for almost 400 years until another major contributor came along. This is not very surprising: mathematics and logic had hardly progressed since the days of Euclid and we were still a long way from the introduction of the printing press which would enable the rapid dissemination of books and knowledge. Europe was still hampered by having nothing better than Roman numerals to perform calculations with, and it should perhaps be no surprise that the man responsible for replacing them by the Arabic numbers with which we are now familiar was also the greatest puzzler of his time.

This man was Leonardo of Pisa, now better known as Fibonacci, which is the name associated with his famous sequence 1, 1, 2, 3, 5, 8, 13, 21 ... of which each number is the sum of the two preceding it. As well as having some remarkable mathematical properties, the Fibonacci sequence has various biological applications, particularly in the realm of population growth. The earliest reference to this sequence appears in a book called *Liber Abaci* (The Book of Calculation) written by Fibonacci in 1202 and forms our Puzzle 6.

? PUZZLE 6

A man keeps a pair of rabbits at a certain place surrounded by a wall. If the nature of these rabbits is that each pair gives birth to one new pair every month and they begin to breed in the second month after their birth, how many rabbits will there be after a year? You are to assume that rabbits never die or become infertile.

Born around 1175 to a wealthy Italian merchant called Guglielmo Bonacci, the man we now know as Fibonacci (that name was only coined in the 1830s as a contraction of *filius Bonacci*, 'son of Bonacci') was probably the finest mathematician of his age. His skills were noticed by the Holy Roman Emperor, Frederick II, who had a strong interest in maths and science. Indeed, it is said that, during the Sixth Crusade, he sent some maths problems to the Muslim forces as a token of cultural friendship. Back in Italy, he ran maths contests, which his team usually won, thanks to the inclusion of Fibonacci.

In 1240, the Republic of Pisa rewarded Fibonacci with a salary for advising the city on matters of accountancy and giving general mathematical instruction to its citizens. In terms of the history of puzzles, he continued very much in the style of Alcuin by setting problems of maths and logic in everyday terms that his readers could relate to. Here are three more from his *Liber Abaci*:

❓ PUZZLE 7

Two birds start flying from the tops of two towers 50 feet apart; one tower is 30 feet high and the other 40 feet high. Starting at the same time and flying at the same rate, the birds reach a fountain between the bases of the towers at the same moment. How far is the fountain from each tower?

❓ PUZZLE 8

A merchant doing business in Lucca doubled his money there and then spent 12 denarii. On leaving, he went to Florence, where he also doubled his money, then spent 12 denarii. Returning home to Pisa, he there doubled his money and again spent 12 denarii, and nothing remained. How much did he have in the beginning?

❓ PUZZLE 9

Three men, each having a number of denarii, found a purse containing 23 denarii. The first man said to the second, 'If I take this purse, I will have twice as much as you.' The second said to the third, 'If I take this purse, I will have three times as much as you.' The third man said to the first, 'If I take this purse, I will have four times as much as you.' How many denarii did each man have?

I could have said 'pence' or 'cents' instead of 'denarii' but that would have lost some of the antiquarian feeling.

'A good clue [in a crossword puzzle] can give you all the pleasure of being duped that a mystery story can. It has surface innocence, surprise, the revelation of a concealed meaning, and the catharsis of solution.'

Stephen Sondheim, *New York* magazine, 8 April 1968

2

PARISIAN PERPLEXITIES, PROBLEMS AND POSERS

ONE OF THE puzzles about puzzles is where the word 'puzzle' came from. The *Oxford English Dictionary* lists it as 'of unknown origin' and traces the verb 'to puzzle' back to around 1595, with the noun following a few years later. Shakespeare's three uses of 'puzzle' (once each in *Antony and Cleopatra, Hamlet* and *Twelfth Night*) all employ it as a verb, although other writers in the early seventeenth century used it as a noun meaning perplexity or bewilderment.

The *Oxford English Dictionary* lists the earliest known use of the word 'puzzle' meaning 'something devised or made for the purpose of testing one's ingenuity' in a citation from 1781, so any puzzles from before then were not called puzzles at all. In the fourteenth century, they were 'problems' or 'conclusions'; in the fifteenth century, they were 'opposals', 'divinaids' or 'riddlings'; in the sixteenth century, a puzzle was a 'why', an 'enigma' or a 'remblere'. After that, the word 'puzzle' gradually became the generic term for the type of mental teasers we know today, although we had to wait until the 1920s before the terms 'brain-twister', 'brain-teaser' and 'skull-buster' arrived, all originating in the United States.

The invention of the printing press greatly enhanced

the spread of puzzles, and a number of early collections proved to be very popular. In France in 1612, the poet and scholar Claude-Gaspar Bachet de Méziriac published a collection of puzzles from earlier manuscripts under the title *Problèmes plaisans et delectables* (Pleasant and Delectable Problems) that proved to be a seventeenth-century bestseller despite the extremely long-winded explanations he gave for the solutions. A large portion of the book is devoted to various tricks in which one is invited to think of a number, then perform a series of arithmetical calculations on it before giving the final answer to the puzzle-setter from which he deduces what your original number was. Both in these think-of-a-number tricks and the other logical puzzles, Bachet explains his methods and answers in tedious detail, through an apparent distrust of his readers' understanding of algebra.

Several of the problems in his book have become classics, such as the two that follow. The second is a wonderful example of seventeenth-century political incorrectness.

❓ PUZZLE 10

What is the least number of weights that would make possible the weighing of any integral number of pounds from 1 pound to 40 pounds inclusive if you can put the weights on either pan of a standard balance?

? PUZZLE 11

In a storm, a ship carrying 15 Christians and 15 Turks as passengers could be saved only by throwing half the passengers into the sea. The passengers were to be placed in a circle, and every  ninth man, beginning at a certain point, was to be cast overboard. How should they be arranged so that all the Christians would be saved?

The first of those two puzzles had in fact already been given by Fibonacci and the second by the sixteenth-century Italian mathematician Niccolò Tartaglia.

Another popular collection of puzzles published in the seventeenth century was a book by Henry van Etten, which first appeared in French in 1624, then in English in 1633 with the ponderous title *Mathematical Recreations; or, a Collection of Sundrie Excellent Problems Extracted out of Ancient and Modern Phylosophers as Secrets and Experiments in arithmetick, geometry, cosmography, horologiography, astronomy, navigation, musick, opticks, architecture, statick, mechanicks, chymistry, water-works, fire-works &c.* Henry van Etten was, in fact, the pseudonym of the Frenchman Jean Leurechon (1591–1670) who was a mathematician, Jesuit priest, and the man who coined the word 'thermometer', which first appeared in his book of puzzles. The book, like that of Bachet, contained a collection of mathematical and scientific tricks, such as his Problem III: 'To tell how much weighs the blow of one's fist, of a Mallet, Hatchet or such like', but also includes some problems that would be recognized by today's puzzle enthusiasts. Here is one example of a type that is still popular, given as his Problem IX.

? PUZZLE 12

How to part a vessel which is full of 8 pints of wine into two equal parts using only two other vessels containing 5 pints and 3 pints.

Thanks to Bachet, van Etten and others, the idea of recreational mathematics had taken such firm root by the end of the seventeenth century that many of the greatest mathematicians of the time adopted puzzle formats to express their ideas. Even Isaac Newton himself expressed some of his ideas in puzzle format, including this example from a series of lectures he gave to students in the 1690s.

❓ PUZZLE 13

In 4 weeks, 12 oxen graze bare 3 and ⅓ acres of meadow, and in 9 weeks, 21 oxen graze bare 10 acres of meadow. Accounting for the uniform growth rate of grass and assuming equal quantities of grass per acre when the pastures are put into use, how many oxen will it take to graze bare 24 acres of meadow in a period of 18 weeks?

This is much trickier than it may seem at first sight. From the opening figure, one may calculate that 12 cows will graze 10 acres in 12 weeks, so 16 oxen ought to manage 10 acres in 12 x 12/16 weeks, which is 9 weeks, and that is when you realize that you haven't taken account of the fact that the grass is growing all the time, which is what accounts for the extra 5 oxen needed to clear the meadow. So, what's the answer to Newton's question?

Mathematical recreations may have been the most respectable form of puzzle at the end of the seventeenth century, but not long after came the development of another favourite that remains with us today: the jigsaw puzzle. The first of these was created in 1766 by John

Spilsbury, a British cartographer and engraver who was apprenticed to Thomas Jefferys, the Royal Geographer to King George III.

Spilsbury's bright idea was to paste a map of the world onto wood, then cut the wood into pieces to provide a challenging and ingenious method of teaching geography to children. Spilsbury's 'Dissected Maps', as he called them, remained popular in schools for almost 150 years before such puzzles began to be mass-produced for adults using a wide variety of pictures instead of maps. These began to appear in the first decade of the twentieth century, and by 1909 they were generally known as 'jigsaw puzzles', probably under the influence of the great nineteenth-century puzzle masters who form the theme for our next chapter.

'I have always treated and considered puzzles from an educational standpoint, for the reason that they constitute a species of mental gymnastics which sharpen the wits and train the mind to reason along straight lines.'

Sam Loyd, Preface, *Cyclopedia of Puzzles*, 1914

3

GREAT VICTORIAN PUZZLERS

?

As **the Industrial** Revolution gathered momentum in the nineteenth century, people's leisure time increased and their appetite for things to do and for things to think about grew. The do-ers were responsible for a huge growth in the popularity of sports, while the thinkers wanted puzzles to fill their time. The groundwork for the Puzzling Revolution, however, began to be set a century earlier in an unlikely-sounding publication.

The *Ladies' Diary or Woman's Almanack* was an annual publication that was founded in 1704 and ran until 1841 when, in a spirit of sexual equality rare for its time, it was succeeded by *The Lady's and Gentleman's Diary*. The very earliest editions were filled mainly with recipes and articles about health, education and notable women, but mathematical puzzles soon became a major feature. The earliest of these were maths problems set by its first editor John Tipper but they soon included puzzles sent in by readers as well. Some were riddles or other word puzzles termed 'enigmas' but many were maths problems which would not be out of place in A-level examinations or even higher. If the idea was to provide puzzles that would last all year until the next edition, it probably succeeded.

In 1709, Tipper wrote: 'Arithmetical Questions are as entertaining and delightful as any other Subject whatever, they are no other than Enigmas to be solved by Numbers', and a few years later, when Tipper died and a new editor took over, they became even more difficult. As well as calling itself the *Ladies' Diary or Woman's Almanack*, the title page expanded itself in various ways each year. In 1792, for example, it was: *The Ladies' Diary or Woman's Almanack For the Year of Our Lord 1792: being Bissextile or Leap-Year, Containing New Improvements in ARTS and SCIENCES, and many Entertaining PARTICULARS: Designed for the Use and Diversion of the FAIR-SEX.*

One can only speculate on how many members of either sex found it diverting in 1749 to be asked: 'How many acres of the moon's surface are seen enlightened 10 days after her conjunction with the sun?' The answer, incidentally, was supplied by a 'Mr Baker' for the 1750 edition as 3,245,609,437 acres.

Moving ahead to the nineteenth century, three men in particular – two British mathematicians and one American chess-player – played prominent roles in satisfying the growing demand for more genuinely diverting puzzles, and created the genre as we know it today. The first of the British mathematician puzzlers was also a deacon of the Anglican church and an author. His name was Charles Lutwidge Dodgson but, in typical puzzling manner, he translated his first names into Latin to give Carolus Ludovicus, which he then inverted to create the pen name by which he became famous: Lewis Carroll. Under that name, he gained great success and fame as the author of *Alice's Adventures in Wonderland* (written in 1865) and its sequel *Through the Looking-Glass* (1871). Both of those included a good deal of playful logical teasing, but it was his later *Pillow Problems* (1880) and *A Tangled Tale* (1885) that included mathematical and logical puzzles as their main theme.

Both these books were collections of puzzles that had earlier appeared as serials in a magazine called *The Monthly Packet of Evening Readings for Members of the English Church*. Carroll's *Pillow Problems* comprise 72 puzzles in algebra, geometry and probability theory, but the second book is much more Carrollian with the puzzles wrapped up in imaginative storylines with each episode describe as a 'Knot'. Here are the first puzzles in Knot 2 and Knot 10:

❓ PUZZLE 14

The Governor of Kgovjni wants to give a very small dinner party, and invites his father's brother-in-law, his brother's father-in-law, his father-in-law's brother, and his brother-in-law's father. What is the least number of guests?

❓ PUZZLE 15

At a home for war veterans, 70 per cent have lost an eye, 75 per cent an ear, 80 per cent an arm, 85 per cent a leg: what percentage, at least, must have lost all four?

As well as mathematical and logical puzzles, Carroll composed and invented a large number and variety of word puzzles, of which the Word Ladder was the best known and most enduring. The basic idea is to turn one word into another of the same length by changing one letter at a time without altering the order of the others, each change resulting in a legitimate English word. A simple example is provided by changing CAT into DOG: CAT – COT – DOT – DOG.

Another of Carroll's was to turn HEAD into TAIL: HEAD – HEAL – TEAL – TELL – TALL – TAIL.

Here are three more of Carroll's Word Ladders, which he called 'Doublets', for you to try.

? PUZZLE 16

Turn ARMY to NAVY with eight letter changes.

? PUZZLE 17

Turn PIG to STY with five changes.

? PUZZLE 18

Turn FLOUR into BREAD with six changes.

And if you want a really difficult one, here's a topical creation of my own.

? PUZZLE 19

Turn TRUMP into PUTIN with 12 changes. Since this involves some very unusual words, we give the entire ladder with clues to the words used at each step:

TRUMP
walk heavily
vehicles
sides
conditions
shoulder muscle
smears with wax
companies of badgers
curs
bodily skin
attractive girl
cellulose plant body
PUTIN

In a letter to a reader in 1879, Lewis Carroll wrote of one Word Ladder: 'You will find this puzzle very soothing: what doctors call "an alternative", i.e. if you happen to have a headache, it will charm it away: but if you haven't one, it will probably give you one.'

Not all his word puzzles were so successful, however. Among those he contributed to *The Lady* magazine, some were a concoction he called 'syzygies', which involved a rather convoluted way to produce a series transforming one word into another. Any two successive words in a syzygy must have a letter or string of letters in common. He gave the example of turning DOOR into WINDOW via the words pOORest, RESound, UNDo and finally wiNDOw (the capital letters in each case highlight the letters each word has in common with its predecessor). Unfortunately, he never came up with a good and simple scoring system for his syzygies and finally gave them up with these words: 'The difficulties in constructing a really satisfactory set of rules seem almost insuperable.'

Before he abandoned syzygies, however, he gave a very thoughtful introduction to them in one issue of *The Lady* in 1891, which is one of the best explanations of the joy of puzzles: 'Whenever the Philosophy of Puzzles comes to be fully discussed ... one chief merit of that form of recreation will be declared to be that it offers a bribe to the human intellect (just as we bribe with dainty dishes an invalid who has lost his appetite) to exert itself, on however trivial a matter, so as not to spend all its waking hours in simple stagnation. All healthy mental games have the same merit.'

The second great British puzzler of the nineteenth century was Henry Ernest Dudeney, a self-taught mathematician who was fascinated by puzzles from the age of 9 and worked as a clerk in the civil service from the age of 13. This job presumably gave him time to indulge his precocious puzzle-passion and from his childhood onwards he supplemented his income by selling ingenious puzzle compositions to magazines and newspapers. In the early 1900s, he was contributing to a wide variety of magazines including *Tit-Bits*, *Blighty*, *The Queen*, *The Strand*, *Cassell's* and the *Weekly Dispatch*.

In 1907, Dudeney published his collection *The Canterbury Puzzles*, which borrowed Chaucer's idea of a group of travellers on their way to Canterbury, but instead of them telling each other stories, they set their companions problems. This book was followed in 1917 by a new collection called *Amusements in Mathematics* and these two works remained the best-known and most popular puzzle books throughout the first half of the twentieth century. Overleaf are four of Dudeney's puzzles, which give an idea of his ingenuity.

? PUZZLE 20

The Nelson Column: Dudeney spins a tale of a man creating a puzzle after staring at Nelson's Column: 'The height of the shaft of the Nelson column being 200 feet and its circumference 16 feet 8 inches, it is wreathed in a regular spiral garland which passes round it exactly five times. What is the length of the garland?' Dudeney adds: 'It looks rather difficult, but is really remarkably easy.'

? PUZZLE 21

The Spider and the Fly: Inside a rectangular room, measuring 30 feet in length and 12 feet in width and height, a spider is at a point on the middle of one of the end walls, 1 foot from the ceiling; a fly is on the opposite wall, 1 foot from the floor in the centre. What is the shortest distance that the spider must crawl in order to reach the fly, which remains stationary? Of course the spider never drops or uses its web, but crawls fairly.

❓ PUZZLE 22

Two trains start at the same time, one from London to Liverpool, the other from Liverpool to London. If they arrive at their destinations 1 hour and 4 hours respectively after passing one another, how much faster is one train running than the other?

❓ PUZZLE 23

If the end of the world should come on the first day of a new century, can you say what are the chances that it will happen on a Sunday?

While Dudeney demonstrated great versatility in his range of puzzles, believing that, as he put it, 'A good puzzle, like virtue, is its own reward,' there was one type of puzzle that he despised. 'There are puzzles and puzzles,' he wrote, approving of puzzles built upon 'some interesting or informing little principle', but having no time for those 'that conceal no principle whatever – such as a picture cut at random into little bits to be put together again, or the juvenile imbecility known as the "rebus", or "picture puzzle".' These, he announced, 'can be confidently recommended to the feeble-minded'.

When Henry Dudeney began supplying several newspapers and magazines with his principled puzzles, he formed an alliance with an American whose work he greatly admired. That man was Sam Loyd and between them they produced numerous ingenious teasers under the pseudonym 'The Sphinx'. The relationship lasted a year but dissolved in bitterness when Dudeney discovered that Loyd was in the habit of publishing many of Dudeney's own creations without acknowledgement of their true authorship. He may also have harboured some doubts about Loyd, whose work included many ingenious picture puzzles.

Dudeney's daughter Margery was young at the time but later recalled her father so furious at Loyd that she grew frightened and thereafter equated Sam Loyd with the devil. There is no doubt, however, that Loyd was at least Dudeney's equal in puzzle creation. Indeed, in the opinion of many, he was the greatest puzzler not only of his age but of all time. In both ingenuity and range, his output was phenomenal, though it cannot be denied that he displayed a reluctance to acknowledge the origin of some of the puzzles he published.

In Loyd's defence, however, it is worth mentioning that his *Cyclopedia of 5,000 Puzzles, Tricks and Conundrums*, which was published in 1914, identifies many of the puzzles as 'by Sam Loyd', but also frequently gives no indication of authorship. Bearing in mind the antiquity of many puzzles, perhaps he was too unsure of the origin of many of them and thought it best to omit any suggestion of authorship of those he had not created himself.

On the other hand, there is little doubt that Loyd's genius in concocting ingenious puzzles was matched by his talent as a self-publicist. His most famous and most successful item was the 15-Puzzle, which consisted of a 4-by-4 square containing 15 blocks, numbered from 1 to 15, with one empty square into which the neighbouring blocks could be slid (see picture overleaf).

Normally, the numbers start jumbled and the solver's task is to restore them to their natural order, but Loyd's version, which he called the 14-15 Puzzle, began with 1 to 13 in the right order but with the last two blocks, 14 and 15, in reverse order. He offered a $1000 prize to the first person to find a manner of sliding the blocks to restore the natural order and proudly announced that the prize had never been claimed – which was hardly surprising as it is impossible.

In his *Cyclopedia of Puzzles*, Loyd wrote: 'The older inhabitants of Puzzleland will remember how in the early seventies I drove the entire world crazy over a little box of movable pieces which became known as the "14-15 Puzzle",' but that was an exaggeration on several counts. First, the craze was only in the United States; second, it was not in the 'early 70s' but in the 1880s; and third, and most important, it had not been invented by Loyd but by a New York postmaster named Noyes Palmer Chapman in the mid-1870s. There is little doubt, however, that Loyd's spurious offer of a $1000 prize added considerably to his success in marketing the puzzle.

Loyd's interest in puzzles in general stemmed from his fascination with chess, of which he was one of America's leading players. His forays into international competition, however, were rather unsuccessful – he finished only two places above last in the Paris tournament in 1867 – and yet his influence on the development of composed chess problems was immense.

The idea of composing problems with chess pieces is extremely ancient, and chess problems are recorded from a time long before the moves of chess games were preserved. Indeed, there is some evidence that such problems were the main form of chess activity in the game's early days. Chess problems, incidentally, were never called 'puzzles' but always shunned the frivolity suggested by that word, preferring to retain their dignity by being considered as 'problems'.

Many of the earliest chess problems were effectively morality tales, or even came with such tales appended, to show a triumph against apparently insuperable odds or an escape from looming disaster. In ancient Persia, such problems were known as 'Mansuba' (plural: 'Mansubat'), meaning 'arrangement' or 'position'. It is also the word for a fiancée, which I suppose could be seen as a particular type of arrangement.

❓ PUZZLE 24

The position illustrated comes from a tenth-century Arab player and story-teller known as Al-Adli. The tale accompanying it concerns a chess-obsessed prince who gambled away his

fortune at the game to reach a sad state when all he has left to wager is his beautiful wife Dilaram whom he bets on the result of a game which reaches the position shown here. The prince is playing with the white pieces and facing threats of immediate mate by a black rook coming to a2, a8 or b4. You must bear in mind, however, that the game was played by the old chess rules in which queens and bishops had considerably limited powers. A queen can move only one square diagonally, a bishop (known as Alfil) can move only two squares diagonally, jumping over another piece if necessary. The knights, rooks and pawns in the position may be taken as moving according to the familiar modern rules but on reaching the end of the board a pawn must promote to a queen. Seeing her future in jeopardy, Princess Dilaram is said to have called out to her husband: 'Oh Prince, sacrifice your rooks and not your wife!' So how does he save his marriage and snatch victory from the jaws of defeat?

By the time Sam Loyd came along, around a thousand years after Dilaram's chessboard predicament, the art of chess problems had developed considerably, giving far greater difficulty to solvers. What Loyd did, however, was introduce a huge element of fun to his chess problems. Apart from the usual checkmates in a specified number of moves, he made some glorious discoveries such as the following two puzzles.

? PUZZLE 25

What is the shortest possible chess game ending in stalemate?

? PUZZLE 26

What is the shortest possible game ending in stalemate, with all the pieces still on the board?

The solutions are a remarkable 10 moves and 12 moves, respectively, on each side, if you care to take up the challenge.

? PUZZLE 27

For a more conventional Sam Loyd chess puzzle, try this classic, which he gave the title of 'Excelsior' for reasons that only become clear when you have solved it. Here's a hint: Loyd said he

composed this for a friend whom he then invited to indicate the piece least likely to deliver checkmate in the main line. And hey presto! The piece the man nominated was indeed the one that gives mate. It's White to play and mate in five moves.

Let us finish this chapter with two more Sam Loyd classics. The first is one of several variations of Alcuin's old river-crossing dilemma; the second is a typically infuriating Sam Loyd concoction almost guaranteed to turn the brain to jelly as you contemplate its intricacy:

? PUZZLE 28

It is told that four men eloped with their sweethearts, but in carrying out their plan they were compelled to cross a stream in a boat which would hold only two at a time and there is an island in the middle of the stream. It appears that the young men were so extremely jealous that not one of them would permit his prospective bride to remain at any time in the company of any other man or men unless he was also present.

Nor was any of the men to get in the boat alone, when there happened to be a girl alone or on the island or shore, other than the one to whom he was engaged. This feature of the condition looks as if the girls were also jealous and feared that their fellows would run off with the wrong girl if they got a chance. Well, be that as it may, the problem is to guess the quickest way to get the whole party across the river according to the conditions imposed. Let us suppose the river is 200 yards wide, with the island in the middle. How many trips would the boat make to get the four couples safely across in accordance with the stipulations?

❓ PUZZLE 29

The combined ages of Mary and Ann are 44 years, and Mary is twice as old as Ann was when Mary was half as old as Ann will be when Ann is three times as old as Mary was when Mary was three times as old as Ann. How old is Mary?

In quoting that puzzle, with full acknowledgement to Loyd as author, Henry Dudeney added: 'That is all, but can you work it out? If not, ask your friends to help you, and watch the shadow of bewilderment creep over their faces as they attempt to grip the intricacies of the question.'

'Archaeology is like a jigsaw puzzle, except that you can't cheat and look at the box, and not all the pieces are there.'

PUZZLES WORTHY OF THE NAME

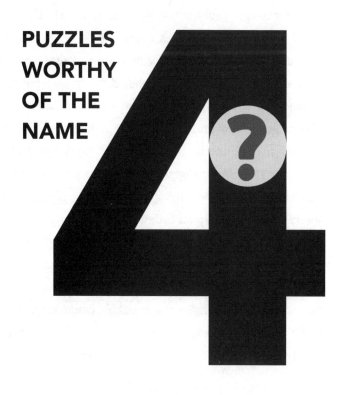

WHAT HAD BEGUN as a way to encourage children to think logically about mathematics had become, thanks to men such as Carroll, Dudeney and Loyd, a major pastime among grown-ups. By the beginning of the twentieth century, every newspaper and magazine was beginning to include a puzzle section but while 'puzzle' had become a generic term for leisure problems, it was not until 1914 that the word became attached to a specific type of puzzle. As already mentioned, the jigsaw had been around for well over a century before anyone called it a 'jigsaw puzzle'. Indeed, the *Oxford English Dictionary* dates a first use of 'jigsaw geography problem' to 1909, followed by 'zigzaw puzzle' in 1912 and its first citation of 'jigsaw puzzle' is not until 1919. Amusingly, this cites the polar explorer Ernest Shackleton describing pack ice as 'a gigantic and interminable jigsaw-puzzle devised by nature', which if nothing else shows the extent to which jigsaws had become part of general experience. Between zigzaw puzzles and jigsaw puzzles, however, we saw the introduction of something that changed the puzzling world, especially as far as daily newspapers were concerned. This was the crossword puzzle. There had been earlier word puzzles, including an Italian sort of crossword in 1890, which had clues to words to be inserted on to a 4-by-4 grid, but there were no shaded squares. Instead, it was Liverpool-born Arthur Wynne (1871–1945) who is generally credited with coming up with the idea we all recognize today as a crossword: a set of interlocking words, across and down, which may be found by solving clues attached to each. It appeared under the name Word-Cross on the Fun page of the comics section of the *New York World* newspaper on 21 December 1913.

As you can see in the image on the next page, unlike modern crosswords, the answers to the clues were to be entered onto a diamond-shaped (rather than rectangular) grid, and the solver was given the word FUN already written as the first entry. Wynne indicated his clues not in the now universal manner as 'across' or 'down', but by giving the locations of the first and last letter. Here they are, so that you may try out the first crossword puzzle.

? PUZZLE 30

2-3. What bargain hunters enjoy.

4-5. A written acknowledgement.

6-7. Such and nothing more.

10-11. A bird.

14-15. Opposed to less.

18-19. What this puzzle is.

22-23. An animal of prey.

26-27. The close of a day.

28-29. To elude.

30-31. The plural of is.

8–9.   To cultivate.

12–13. A bar of wood or iron.

16–17. What artists learn to do.

20–21. Fastened.

24–25. Found on the seashore.

10–18. The fibre of the gomuti palm.

6–22. What we all should be.

4–26. A day dream.

2–11. A talon.

19–28. A pigeon.

F–7.   Part of your head.

23–30. A river in Russia.

1–32. To govern.

33–34. Aromatic plant.

N–8.   A fist.

24–31. To agree with.

3–12. Part of a ship.

20–29. One.

5–27. Exchanging.

9–25. To sink in mud [sic; but 'sunk in mud' is technically correct].

13–21. A boy.

Despite its inclusion of some highly unusual words, such as NEIF, NEVA, NARD and TANE, Wynne's 'Word-Cross' proved very popular and became a regular feature. He can be forgiven for not being familiar with Homer Simpson's all-purpose expression of frustration, but clueing 'DOH' as 'The fibre of the gomuti palm' suggests that he did not know the notes of the tonic solfa 'doh, re, mi' scale either. One wonders how many readers of the *New York World* were familiar with the gomuti palm. The puzzle format, however, did not feature any black squares apart from the diamond shape in the middle, so almost every letter was clued twice, once in an across word and once in a down word, so there were generally two ways to fill in any troublesome gaps.

After a few weeks, apparently due to an error by a typesetter, the name changed from Word-Cross to Cross-Word early in 1914, and this soon became so familiar that it began to be spelt as a single word without a hyphen.

Although Wynne's new puzzle in the *New York World* was highly successful with readers, it was not universally approved of, even in the city of its birth. In 1925, the *New York Times* wrote a strong criticism of crosswords ending: 'Fortunately, the question of whether the puzzles are beneficial or harmful is in no urgent need of an answer. The craze evidently is dying out fast and in a few months it will be forgotten.'

They could hardly have been more wrong. The crossword craze had already spread to Britain, where *Pearson's Magazine* became the first to print a crossword in February 1922, and in 1924 the *Sunday Express* became the first newspaper to do so. In the same year, the first book of crosswords was published in the United States. It had a pencil attached for the benefit of solvers and was an immediate success.

Although Arthur Wynne had emigrated from England to the United States at the age of 19, the British rapidly became world leaders in this field with the introduction of cryptic crosswords in 1925, the first of which appeared in the Saturday *Westminster Gazette.* There had been occasional cryptic clues before that date but now truly puzzling puzzles began to be produced with all the clues cryptic. The Americans continued with mainly straight definitions in their clues until the 1960s, when it is said that the composer Stephen Sondheim, a great enthusiast of all types of puzzle, brought the British style of cryptic crosswords across the Atlantic. Perhaps the biggest puzzle of all, however, came during the Second World War in 1944 when a crossword compiler was hauled before military intelligence on suspicion of giving away secrets.

Answers in this particular newspaper crossword over several days had included Utah, Omaha and Mulberry, all of which were code words in Operation Overlord, which was the plan culminating in the D-Day landings. A few days later Neptune (which was the name given to the naval operations) and Overlord itself appeared in the puzzle. After interviewing the compiler, a schoolteacher named Leonard Dawe, the investigators were satisfied that he was totally innocent of any attempt to pass information to the enemy. It seems he had just heard the words in soldiers' conversations and used them to help fill his grids.

What Wynne had introduced to puzzles, whether consciously or not, was an ingredient that heightened addiction in a highly effective manner. Before crosswords, puzzles were almost exclusively single tasks: you solved one puzzle, then went on afresh to the next one. A crossword posed a series of word problems, but solving each one provided letters that aided the solution of other clues. Many years later, sudoku puzzles became very popular for a similar reason: as you fill in the grid, the overall task is liable to become easier.

It was perhaps no coincidence that the crossword craze of the 1920s coincided with a craze for adult jigsaws. What jigsaws did with shapes, crosswords did with letters; but it took more than another half century before sudokus followed with an addictive completion task based on numbers.

The other main outbreak of twentieth-century puzzle addiction followed the same pattern, but the Rubik's Cube did it with colours. In each case, whether it was jigsaws, crosswords, sudoku or Rubik's Cubes, the nearer you came to completion, the easier finishing the overall task was liable to become.

To finish this chapter, here are some of my favourite cryptic crossword clues to tackle, including some examples of a type that always impresses me: short clues with long answers. For that reason, I give these in reverse order of clue length. As usual, the lengths of the word or words in the answers is given in brackets after the clue. Sadly, I do not know the identity of the tantalizing geniuses who composed these teasers. Crossword compilers, or 'cruciverbalists' as they call themselves, are a shy breed who generally choose to remain anonymous or hide behind ingenious pseudonyms.

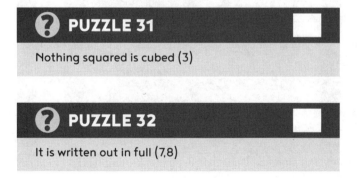

❓ PUZZLE 31

Nothing squared is cubed (3)

❓ PUZZLE 32

It is written out in full (7,8)

❓ PUZZLE 33

Bar of soap (6,6)

❓ PUZZLE 34

HIJKLMNO (5)

❓ PUZZLE 35

BRESH (5,5)

❓ PUZZLE 36

GEGS (9,4)

❓ PUZZLE 37

014 (6,5)

❓ PUZZLE 38

Ca? (4,3)

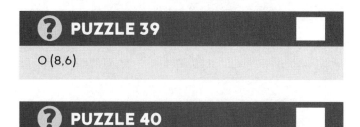

? PUZZLE 39

O (8,6)

? PUZZLE 40

(3,3,3,1,4)

In case of total bemusement, here are some hints: 31. Think of another way to write 'nothing squared'. 32. Putting quotation marks around 'it' should be helpful. 33. Think *Coronation Street*. 34. What's a quick way to say this clue? 35. Try an anagram. 36. Think breakfast. 37. Try dividing by two. 38. The answer has something missing. 39. The shape gives it away. 40. No words express this idea.

'It may be a mere intellectual puzzle to you, but it is life and death to me!'

Sir Arthur Conan Doyle, *The Case-Book of Sherlock Holmes*, 1927

MORE WORD PUZZLES

WHAT DO THE following have in common: the musicians Britney Spears, Eric Clapton, Roger Daltrey and Fats Waller; chess grandmasters Nigel Short and Tony Miles; actors Meg Ryan and Tom Cruise; politician Clare Short; TV personality Steve Irwin?

Hint: Aristotle could join them, and Socrates could do so twice.

❓ PUZZLES 41-52

The answer is that they all have one-word English anagrams of their names, and finding them gives us our Puzzles 41-52 (including Aristotle and Socrates).

Here is another more difficult linguistic word puzzle:

❓ PUZZLE 53

What do the words sine, ride, chess and chat have in common that is shared by riots, pest and zone, but not in the same place?

As with crossword clues, many word puzzles are based on anagrams or similar letter rearrangements, but such puzzles long pre-dated crosswords. Sam Loyd's 1914 *Cyclopedia* includes several varieties of such puzzles, including many riddles in wince-making Christmas cracker style:

When is a fowl's neck like a bell? When it is (w)rung for dinner.

And while we are on the wince-worthy riddles, try this.

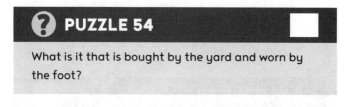

? PUZZLE 54

What is it that is bought by the yard and worn by the foot?

Some of Loyd's word puzzles, such as those above, were nothing more than linguistic jokes, so here are two more of more recent origin.

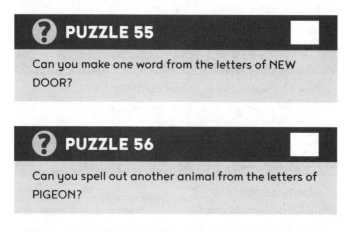

? PUZZLE 55

Can you make one word from the letters of NEW DOOR?

? PUZZLE 56

Can you spell out another animal from the letters of PIGEON?

Many in Loyd's *Cyclopedia*, usually entitled 'rebus' or 'charade', are less groan-worthy, including some word puzzles that may be seen as predecessors of cryptic crossword clues, but with Loyd posing the question in rhymes, such as Puzzles 57 to 60.

? PUZZLE 57

I'm of little importance so off with my head;
To a foe I might then be the terror and dread.
Decapitate twice, and reverse what remains
And lo! you've a wandering sprite for your pains.

? PUZZLE 58

Though of my first the quack may boast
My next he cannot cure;
Who do my whole along the coast
Should punishment endure.

? PUZZLE 59

A word there is five syllables contains;
Take one away, not a single one remains.

? PUZZLE 60

Ladies a riddle I submit:-
To fifty now add one;*
And, having thereby shown your wit,
You may my whole put on.

* In modern crossword terms, this might appear as '50 + 1 may be knotted'.

Of the other two great nineteenth-century puzzlers, Dudeney only rarely dabbled with word puzzles, while as we have seen Carroll delighted in them, introducing word ladders and his syzygies, even though he could never quite get the latter to work. Both Carroll and Loyd also came up with plenty of word squares, featuring a full square of letters forming words that could be read either along the rows or down the columns. A simple example is this:

F	A	I	R
A	L	T	O
I	T	E	M
R	O	M	P

An example of a 6-by-6 square is this:

P	L	E	A	S	E
L	A	R	D	E	R
E	R	R	A	T	A
A	D	A	P	T	S
S	E	T	T	L	E
E	R	A	S	E	D

❓ PUZZLE 61

And here is how Loyd created a puzzle out of a 5-by-5 word square, which he called a 'square word puzzle':

1. A recess

2. A lazy fellow

3. Girl's name

4. Flocks

5. To rub out

Before crosswords came along, there were indeed many different forms of word puzzle such as these, usually based on different ways, verbal or pictorial, of indicating the letters forming a word or its meaning. Crosswords quickly dominated the word puzzle scene by combining all the tricks into one format.

For more than 50 years, crosswords were the only word puzzle that had a universally accepted name, but since the 1970s another has emerged and, in 1999, the new teaser was given a name. The word 'ditloid' is not yet in the *Oxford English Dictionary*, but a Google search for 'ditloid' produces tens of thousands of results. I am delighted by this, because it is a word I coined myself and is my only genuine contribution to the English language.

Ditloids are puzzles of the form '26 L o t A' or '7 D o t

W' or '3 B M (S H T R)', which begin with a number, then challenge you to complete the words of which only the initial letters are given. In the examples above, lower case letters are used for common short words such as articles or prepositions, with capital letters for the main elements. Some setters like to give the short words in full, others add to the confusion by giving everything in capitals. The answers to the examples are '26 Letters of the Alphabet', '7 Days of the Week', '3 Blind Mice (See How They Run)'.

These are among the easier ones. An early version of these was included in a book by the American psychologist Morgan Worthy, published in 1975 under the title *Aha! A Puzzle Approach to Creative Thinking*. He starts the book with a 'Formula Analysis Test', consisting of items such as 'N.N. = G.N.' (No News is Good News) or '8P = 1G' (8 Pints = 1 Gallon) designed to illustrate the flash of creative insight – which he called the aha! moment – which comes on finding the solution to such a puzzle.

In 1999, the *Daily Express* newspaper began publishing a short-lived Puzzle supplement and I was invited to contribute various items. These alphanumeric word puzzles were high on my list of suggestions, but they needed a name. And that's when 'ditloid' flashed into my mind. It first appeared in print on 29 October 1999. It's perfect really, as you will see when you solve the second of the following set.

? PUZZLE 62

OLiT

? PUZZLE 63

1DitLoID

? PUZZLE 64

2BoCiaM

? PUZZLE 65

3BiG

? PUZZLE 66

4LoaLC

? PUZZLE 67

5ToaF

PUZZLE 68

6 H a D

PUZZLE 69

7 E i a H

PUZZLE 70

8 E T C

PUZZLE 71

9 L o a C

PUZZLE 72

10 D S

And if you want a really difficult one:

PUZZLE 73

29 L i F

I once included Puzzle 73 in an especially difficult newspaper Christmas competition. I was delighted and very impressed when more than one reader got the right answer.

'Logic: The art of thinking and reasoning in strict accordance with the limitations and incapacities of the human misunderstanding.'

Ambrose Bierce, *The Devil's Dictionary*, 1906

THE LOGIC OF HATS

I N HIS *536 Puzzles and Curious Problems* collection, published in 1931, Henry Dudeney introduced a type of puzzle that became very popular in the 1950s and 1960s. Because of the original one of these problems, they were referred to by many as 'Smith–Robinson–Jones' puzzles:

Three businessmen – Smith, Robinson and Jones – all live in the Leeds–Sheffield district. Three railwaymen with the same names live in the same district. The businessman Robinson and the guard live in Sheffield, the businessman Jones and the stoker live in Leeds, while the businessman Smith and the railway engineer live halfway between Leeds and Sheffield. The guard's namesake earns £10,000 per annum, and the engineer earns exactly one-third as much as the businessman living nearest to him. Finally, the railwayman Smith beat the stoker at billiards. What is the engineer's name?

The only difficulty in solving this is the danger of confusing the businessmen with the railwaymen of the same names. The guard cannot be named Smith for the following reason: the businessman Smith (who would then be the guard's namesake) earns £10,000 a year and is the engineer's nearest neighbour (as they both live halfway between Leeds and Sheffield) but £10,000 is not exactly divisible by three. But railwayman Smith beat the stoker at billiards, so Smith is also not the name of the stoker. The only possibility left is that Smith is the engineer. We don't know which of the guard and stoker is Jones and which is Robinson, but that is not what the question asks.

As more Smith–Robinson–Jones puzzles began to be created, they all became known by the generic term 'logic puzzles', and grew more and more complex. In principle, they could all be solved by drawing grids of the possibilities and eliminating those that were excluded in the ever more elaborate conditions that typically involved people named Mrs Green, Mrs Black, Mrs White and Mrs Brown, wearing green, black, white and brown dresses (but never matching their names) and living in green, black, white and brown houses with green, black, white and brown doors.

Here is a slightly different variation on the theme:

❓ PUZZLE 74

Five criminals named Mr Arson, Mr Battery, Mr Conspiracy, Mr Drunkendriving and Mr Murder all appeared before a court for sentence, having been convicted of the crimes of arson, battery, conspiracy, drunken-driving and murder, although in no cases did the crime match the name of the convict.

The person bearing the name of the crime with which Mr Conspiracy was charged was himself charged with the crime of which the namesake was charged with murder.

The person bearing the name of the crime with which Mr Murder was charged was himself charged with the crime of which the namesake was charged with arson.

All received jail terms, including Mr Drunkendriving, except the man charged with murder who was sentenced to death. Who was the murderer?

As puzzlers began to tire of ticking off possibilities on grids, logic puzzles entered a more varied, more mind-blowing and generally more amusing phase, and that is where the hats came in. It all started around 1960 with a neat little puzzle concerning three logicians and five hats.

Three logicians are blindfolded and taken into a room where it is explained to them that there are three white hats and two black hats. Each logician will be fitted with a hat; the two unused hats will then be hidden and the blindfolds will be removed. Each can then see the colour of the other two men's hats but not their own.

The first logician is then asked: 'Do you know the colour of your hat?' and he says, 'No.'

The second logician is then asked: 'Do you know the

colour of your hat?' and he says, 'No.'

The third logician is then asked: 'Do you know the colour of your hat?' and he says, 'No.'

The first logician is then asked again: 'Do you know the colour of your hat?'

What does he say and what are the colours of the three hats?

The point of this puzzle is that each of the logicians, whom we shall call A, B and C, assumes the others are thinking rationally. There were three white hats and two black hats to choose from at the start, so if A sees two black hats, he knows his must be white. When he says that he does not know what colour hat he is wearing, the others may deduce that they are not both wearing black. When B then also says he does not know what colour hat he is wearing, we know that C does not have a black hat, for if he did then B would know his own hat must be white. We have thus eliminated the possibilities WBB, BWB and WWB. The inability of C to name his colour then eliminates both BBW and WBW, for the first would tell C his hat must be white, and the second also identifies C's hat as white, for if it were black then A would have known his own colour immediately. So, when C says 'No', that leaves only the possibility that all are wearing white hats.

That logical puzzle, which dates back to around 1961, then led to some intriguing variations. Try this one.

❓ PUZZLE 75

Three logicians, A, B and C, are again wearing black or white hats, but this time all they are told is that they are not all white. A can see the hats of B and C; B can see the hats of A and C; but logician C is blind. As usual, they are asked in turn if they know the colour of their own hat. The answers are:

A: 'No.'

B: 'No.'

C: 'Yes.'

What colour was the blind logician's hat and how did he know?

And finally, before we leave hats, let's don some headgear for a whole convention of logicians.

❓ PUZZLE 76

There are 50 logicians attending a conference, and to keep them amused on a free evening, they are all given black or white hats and, of course, they cannot see their own hats. All they are told is that at least one of them has a white hat. In fact, although they do not know it, all of them have white hats. They are told that a prize awaits the first to correctly identify that he is wearing a white hat. A wrong claim, of course, will lead to the ignominy of being expelled from the Logicians' Union. They are placed in a room with the light turned off. The light is briefly turned on, then off again. When, after a few seconds, nobody claims the prize, the light is turned on and off again, and this procedure continues until someone says that he is wearing a white hat. Explain what happens.

Having solved that puzzle, you should be able to do this one, which is essentially a hatless version of the same thing.

? PUZZLE 77

The vicar of a religious community is appalled at the amount of adultery going on among his parishioners who comprise 50 married couples. One Sunday, he announces in his sermon that there is at least one adulterer among the husbands, and any wife who discovers that her husband is unfaithful should kick him out of the town.

The women, however, are blissfully ignorant of their own husbands' amorous adventures, although they know all the other men in the town are adulterers. So, the following Sunday, they all turn up at church, look around to see who has been kicked out, and discover that all the husbands are present. What happens next?

Another similar variety of puzzle involves logicians with various things drawn on their foreheads, which allows greater versatility than hats.

One version features three people with numbers written on their foreheads. They are told that all the numbers are positive, non-zero integers and that one of the numbers is the sum of the other two. Each can see the other two numbers, but not their own. As usual, they are asked if they know their number.

As a simple example, think about what happens when A is given the number 1, B is 2, C is 3. A sees 2 and 3, so reasons that his number is 1 or 5, but he cannot tell which. B knows that his is 2 or 4, but cannot say which. C then reasons that his number must be 1 or 3, but if it were 1, then B would have seen 1 and 1, and known that his own number must be 2, as zero is not allowed. So C's number must be 3.

It's a bit more complex if A, B, C have 1, 3, 2 respectively. A cannot tell if he has 1 or 5; B cannot tell if he has 1 or 3; C could be 2 or 4. So they have to go round again. A still does not know whether he is 1 or 5 but B now knows his must be 3 because, if it were 1, then C would have seen two 1s and known that his number must be 2.

In fact, whatever three numbers are chosen, with one being the sum of the other two, one person will eventually be able to work out what his is, assuming that the others are thinking logically. As the numbers get larger, however, the process can be extended longer and longer. Try this for a really tricky one.

? PUZZLE 78

In the usual three numbers scenario, with one being the sum of the other two, all three logicians cannot tell their number on the first round. Then A says 'No' again and B correctly says his number is 13. What are the other two numbers?

A slightly easier puzzle features not numbers but coloured stamps on foreheads.

? PUZZLE 79

Three logicians are each told that they will have two coloured stamps stuck on their foreheads. The stamp-sticker says that he has four blue stamps and four yellow ones. After using six of them, he hides the two he has not used. The logicians then, as usual, see the others' stamps and are asked if they can deduce their own. A says 'No', then B says 'No', then C says 'No'. A can still not say what colour stamps he has, but B now says he knows. What are B's stamps?

Finally, here are a couple of hat questions which I think are the best of all. The first is a surprising test of logic; the second is my own variation of it, which I think has an even more surprising answer.

❓ PUZZLE 80

An evil warlord has captured 100 prisoners, some of whom, he says, will be executed in the morning. They will all be placed in a long line so that each can see only those in front of him in the line. They will all be given either black or white hats, and they can see all the hats in front of them but not their own or the ones behind them. One by one, starting at the back of the line, they are asked to guess the colour of their own hat. If they get it right, they are freed; if they get it wrong, they are beheaded immediately.

On the night before the execution, the prisoners must find a strategy that saves the highest possible number of them. How many can they save and what's the strategy?

❓ PUZZLE 81

Feeling himself cheated by their chosen strategy, the next time he has 100 prisoners, the warlord equips himself with many red hats as well as the black and white ones. The rules are the same as before. How many can now be saved?

If you can solve that one, you will probably be able to work out what happens with even more colours of hats.

'Contrariwise, if it was so, it might be; and if it were so, it would be; but as it isn't, it ain't. That's logic.'

Lewis Carroll, *Alice's Adventures in Wonderland*, 1865

7

THE MOST BAFFLING LOGIC OF ALL

THE PREVIOUS CHAPTER referred to the genre of logic puzzles, which dates back almost a century. In the 1970s, however, there emerged a true logician-puzzler who raised this subject to a real art. Raymond Smullyan (1919–2017) was a stage magician, a concert pianist, a mathematician and a philosopher who had the knack of taking simple logic puzzles and turning them into something truly baffling and entertaining.

As an example of how Smullyan's mind worked, consider this story concerning his first meeting with his future wife. Like him, she was a concert pianist and after one of her recitals, he said to her: 'I am about to make a statement. If the statement is true, will you give me your autograph, but not give me your autograph if it is false?'

The woman agreed, so he made his statement: 'You'll give me neither your autograph nor a kiss.'

She was trapped. If the statement was true, she must give him her autograph, which makes the statement false, but the statement can only be false if she gives him an autograph or a kiss. But she can't give him an autograph because the statement is false, so she has to kiss him.

Smullyan's first book of puzzles appeared in 1978 under the title *What Is the Name of This Book?* and he wrote *The Lady or the Tiger* in 1982; in both these books Smullyan applied his devious mind to turn older ideas into glorious exercises in logic. In between these publications, he wrote two books of highly unusual chess problems on the theme of retro-analysis, dealing not with the usual fare of what happens next in a given position, but the question of what had happened before to lead to that state.

Here is one remarkably simple-looking position from *The Chess Mysteries of Sherlock Holmes.*

❓ PUZZLE 82

As you may have noticed, there is no white king in the position so the question is simple: if White's king is the only piece missing from the position, where is it and how did it get there?

Notice that, unless the white king is on b3, Black is in check from the bishop, but White's king cannot be on b3 without being in an impossible double-check from both rook and bishop. So Black is indeed in check, which raises the question of how that is possible with the white bishop's path to a4 being blocked by the rook.

Most of Smullyan's chess positions are more complex, so let's have just one more before proceeding to his logic puzzles.

❓ PUZZLE 83

White's first four moves in a game were 1.f3, 2.Kf2, 3.Kg3, 4.Kh4, whereupon Black delivered immediate mate on his own fourth move. What were Black's moves?

Smullyan's book *The Lady and the Tiger* took its theme and title from a short story written by the American writer and humorist Frank Stockton in 1882. The story featured a land ruled by a king who instigated an ingenious mode of trial for men accused of a crime. The defendant had to choose to open one of two doors. One concealed a woman whom the king had chosen as a potential wife for the man, but the other hid a fierce and hungry tiger. If he chose the right door, he was deemed innocent and got to marry the woman, but if he chose the wrong door he was eaten by the tiger.

Smullyan adopted the door-choosing method of the story, but created a more meritocratic king who decided that logical ability should be rewarded. He did not promise that there would be one lady and one tiger but said that there might be two of either; however, he attached signs to the two doors, which form the basis for our next three puzzles.

? PUZZLE 84

The sign on Room A reads: 'In this room there is a lady but in the other room there is a tiger.' The sign on Room B says: 'In one of these rooms there is a lady and in the other there is a tiger.' The king informs the man that one of these signs is true, but the other is false. Which should he choose?

? PUZZLE 85

This time the signs were changed. Room A says: 'At least one of these rooms contains a lady.' Room B says: 'A tiger is in the other room', and this time the king told the man that either both signs were right or both were wrong.

? PUZZLE 86

Again, the man is told that the signs are either both true or both false. This time Room A says: 'Either a tiger is in this room or a lady is in the other room,' while Room B says: 'A lady is in the other room.'

It's time for a short break from Smullyan's mind-melting puzzles to allow our brains to set again, so here are a couple of more mundane riddles:

? PUZZLE 87

A man buys a parrot in a pet shop which the owner has assured him will repeat any word it hears. On getting the parrot home and talking to it, however, the man is rewarded with total silence. So he takes the parrot back to the shop and demands a refund. The pet shop owner refuses, on the grounds that what he said was perfectly true. Explain.

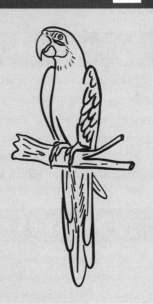

? PUZZLE 88

If two's company and three's a crowd, what is four and five?

Let's return from riddle ridiculous to the sublimeness of Smullyan. Some of his best logical problems stemmed not from a short story but from an old puzzle about a liar and a truth-teller. I believe that they originally took the form of two guards at a fork in the road. One direction led to heaven, the other to hell and a traveller is permitted to ask only one question of only one of the guards. The trouble is that one of them always tells the truth, the other always lies and the traveller does not know which is which.

There are several possible solutions, of which the usual one given is to point to one of the guards and ask the other one, 'Which road would your companion say leads to heaven?' Whichever road is given as the answer, the traveller should then take the other one. Even simpler, the traveller could ask: 'What answer would you give if I asked which road leads to heaven?' and then follow the answer given.

Smullyan hugely developed this theme, dropping the heaven and hell tale but setting his logical dilemmas on an island populated by knights, who always tell the truth, and knaves, who always lie. In his 1987 book *Forever Undecided*, he uses this puzzle approach to explain and prove Gödel's incompleteness theorem, which was one of the most complex and far-reaching discoveries in logic and philosophy in the twentieth century. Despite his light-hearted approach, Smullyan's book soon veers into the language and symbolism of propositional logic, but to introduce the reader to ideas of truth, falsehood and unprovability, he starts with a few knight and knave puzzles. Here are three early examples.

? PUZZLE 89

A census taker on the island of knights and knaves asks a householder for information about himself and his wife: 'Which, if either of you, is a knight and which is a knave?' The man angrily says, 'We are both knaves.' What conclusions can the census taker draw?

? PUZZLE 90

At another house, he asks the husband: 'Are both of you knaves?', and receives the reply: 'At least one of us is.' What types are they?

? PUZZLE 91

The most complex answer he received, however, was from a man who said: 'If I am a knight, then so is my wife.' Is this enough to tell what they both are?

Back on the original question of the guards at a fork in the road, Smullyan and his followers brilliantly complicated the issue by introducing the idea of a third guard who answers completely at random. Here is one such puzzle.

? PUZZLE 92

You come to a fork in the road where you know that one way leads to heaven, the other to hell. There are three guards, a truth-teller, a liar, and one who answers at random. You are allowed only two questions to find the right road, each addressed to only one guard. The guards know each other's identities. What do you ask?

If that was not difficult enough, here's one which has been described by several writers as 'the most difficult logic puzzle ever'.

? PUZZLE 93

Again, you meet three men whom you know to be a truth-teller, a liar, and one who answers at random. This time, your task is not to find the right road but to determine which man is which. You have three questions, each addressed to a man of your choice, but to add to the difficulty, you do not speak their language. You know their words 'ja' and 'na' mean either 'yes' or 'no' but you do not know which is 'yes' and which is 'no'. So how do you solve the problem?

In one formulation of this problem, the three men are cast as gods, but I doubt that any god would be so infuriatingly logical.

'The problems of puzzles are very near the problems of life, our whole life is solving puzzles.'

Erno Rubik

WEIGHTS, MEASURES AND SPEEDS

8

PUZZLE-SETTERS, FROM THE earliest days, have been attracted by the idea of setting puzzles in ways that are relevant to the solvers. The pure mathematics or logic behind them is expressed in terms of weights of goods, or volumes of liquids, or times taken for journeys; and counterfeit coins, jars of wine, and cars or trains were all involved in their own genres of puzzle.

One such set of puzzles concerns finding the counterfeit coin in a group. In its simplest form, you are told that the fake coin is known to be underweight and you must determine which one it is by making a series of trials, putting various numbers of coins in the two trays of a balance. The question is: what is the maximum number of coins for which you can determine the single underweight one in only two weighings?

You can arrive at the answer by realizing that you can find the fake among three coins in only one weighing. Just weigh coin A against coin B. If they balance, then coin C must be the fake; if they do not balance, then the coin that is left in the air while the other one sinks must be the underweight fake we are looking for.

So with nine coins, we divide them into three groups of three, then weigh A+B+C against D+E+F. If they balance, it means that the fake must be among the other three; if they do not balance, the fake is in the lighter group. In either case, we are left with three candidates which, as we have seen, need only one weighing.

This quickly leads to a solution of how many weighings are needed for any group of coins. Three weighings are enough for 27 coins, four for 81 coins, five for 243 and so on, going up in powers of three.

The problem, however, becomes much trickier if we do not know whether the fake is heavier or lighter than the good coins.

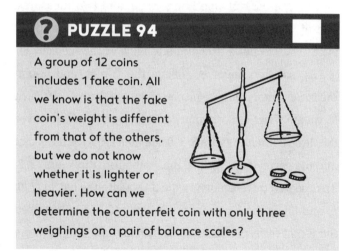

❓ PUZZLE 94

A group of 12 coins includes 1 fake coin. All we know is that the fake coin's weight is different from that of the others, but we do not know whether it is lighter or heavier. How can we determine the counterfeit coin with only three weighings on a pair of balance scales?

Here is another weighing puzzle that befuddled several competitors at the Moscow Mathematical Olympiad in 1991. It was composed by Sergei Tokarev.

❓ PUZZLE 95

There are 6 weights of 1, 2, 3, 4, 5 and 6 grams that look identical, except for their labels which number them from 1 to 6, but not necessarily in the right order. Using the balance scale only twice, how can we determine whether the labels are on the right weights or whether an error has occurred?

Moving from weights to wine, Dudeney, in *The Canterbury Puzzles*, tells the tale of The Host's Puzzle, where the innkeeper of The Tabard poses a puzzle involving a cask of fine London ale, and two measures, one of 5 pints, and the other of 3 pints. He asks how it is possible 'to put a true pint into each of the measures'.

His solution involved filling the 5-pint and 3-pint measures, then – despite protests – letting the barrel (which fortunately was almost empty anyway) run dry. This leaves the three containers with 5, 3, 0. He then emptied the 3-pint into the barrel (5, 0, 3), filled the 3-pint from the 5-pint (2, 3, 3), repeated this – emptying the 3-pint into the barrel (2, 0, 6) and filling the 3-pint from the 5-pint (0, 2, 6), then filled the 5-pint from the barrel (5, 2, 1) and the 3-pint from the 5-pint (4, 3, 1), then let the company drink the contents of the 3-pint leaving (4, 0, 1), filled the 3-pint from the 5-pint (1, 3, 1), then drank the 3-pint, and finally poured the 1 pint from the barrel into the 3-pint measure.

That solved the problem, but only after several pints had been drunk or wasted along the way. Later puzzlers have preferred not to be so profligate with their ale, so provide enough jugs or casks to fulfil the tasks without waste. Here are a couple more examples to solve, the first reasonably straightforward, taking 6 steps to reach the desired state, while the second needs 16.

❓ PUZZLE 96

You have one 4-pint, one 7-pint and one 9-pint container, as well as a large barrel. You want to end with just 1 pint in each of the two smallest containers.

❓ PUZZLE 97

You have a 4-pint, a 7-pint and a 22-pint container, as well as the barrel. Again, you want to end with just 1 pint in each of the two smallest containers.

To end this section of puzzles built around everyday life, let us take a trip into the sometimes paradoxical maths of travel. To get in the mood, try this easy one:

A man drives to work in the morning rush hour when, because of the usual delays and congestion, he can manage an average speed of only 10 miles per hour. How fast must he drive along the same route when returning home in order to bring his average speed for the whole journey there and back up to 20 miles per hour?

Think about this carefully, and if you still end up with an answer of 30 miles per hour, on the grounds that 20 is the average of 10 and 30, then think again.

The right answer is that the poor fellow cannot possibly get his average up to 20 miles per hour. Suppose, for the sake of simplicity, the distance from home to work is 10 miles, then it takes him an hour to get there. To go there and back would be a total of 20 miles, and to cover that at an average speed of 20 miles per hour would allow him only an hour for both journeys. In other words, he would have to get home in no time at all.

With that in mind, try to steer clear of the traps in the following puzzles. The first is an old Russian puzzle, while the second offers a very simple route to the solution or a much more complicated one. See if you can find the simple way.

? PUZZLE 98

Two motorcyclists made exactly the same journey and took exactly the same time, but the first motorcyclist rode for twice as long as the second one rested, while the second one rode for three times as long as the first one rested. Which one rode faster?

❓ PUZZLE 99

Two slow trains start at the same time, one from London to Birmingham, the other from Birmingham to London, both travelling the 100-mile journey at a speed of 25 miles per hour. A dragonfly is sitting on the front of one train when it starts and is so startled that it flies off at its top speed of 35 miles per hour and heads down the track towards the other train.

When it reaches the other train, it turns around and heads back towards the first one and it continues the process, reversing whenever it meets the other train and never changing its speed. How far in total will the dragonfly have flown when the trains meet?

Of course, if either of those scenarios had been scheduled around the time of the great timetable change on the UK rail network in 2018, the trains involved would in all probability have been cancelled and the dragonfly would have saved a lot of effort. However, the resulting delays gave me time to compose the following puzzle.

? PUZZLE 100

In the following sum, each letter represents a distinct digit. Can you find out what they are?

```
      TRAIN
+     TRAIN
   _____
     CANCEL
```

And while we are on the subject of letters substituted for numbers, can you work out these two?

? PUZZLE 101

```
     LUNACY
+    LUNACY
+    LUNACY
   _____
     ASYLUM
```

And the considerably more difficult Puzzle 102.

? PUZZLE 102

```
        MAD
x       MAN
     _____
     ASYLUM
```

All this train cancellation and craziness calls for a more sedate car journey, so try this one.

? PUZZLE 103

A woman has the choice of driving to work or going by bus. The bus service is regular and reliable but rather slow. In fact, when driving to work, she notices that she always overtakes exactly 8 buses going the same way. When she comes back home, however, she meets 16 buses going in the opposite direction. Her journey in either direction takes exactly 1 hour. Assuming the buses set off at the same regular intervals in both directions and that interval remains constant all day, how often do buses run?

Just in case all these calculations about cars, trains and buses make you want to walk to work, let's end this section on foot.

? PUZZLE 104

A man walks down an escalator towards a tube train, reaching the bottom in 1 minute. He then realizes that he has left his briefcase at the top of the escalator. As the upward escalators are on the other side of the station, he decides to walk up the same down escalator. Fortunately, his walking speed is faster than that of the escalator and he reaches the top in 3 minutes and retrieves his case. Rather tired from all that exercise, he then stands still and lets the escalator carry him down. How long does it take?

Surprisingly, it only complicates the issue to tell you the length of escalator or its speed or that of the man.

'The unfortunate inmates of our lunatic asylums are sent there expressly because they cannot solve puzzles – because they have lost their powers of reason.'

H. E. Dudeney, Preface,
Amusements in Mathematics, 1917

9

PSYCHOLOGICAL PUZZLES

WHAT IS THE difference between a puzzle and an intelligence test item? The answer, I suppose, is that puzzles are fun – or at least they are meant to be. Finding the right answer to an IQ question demands basic reasoning ability; a good puzzle asks for more than that and the best ones require also at least a small leap in imagination to solve them, and a bit of wit in their composition. This chapter includes some puzzles that could easily be mistaken for intelligence test items but include ideas specifically designed to throw the solver off course.

One puzzle-type question above all has fascinated psychologists for more than half a century, the reason being that solving it appears to be purely a matter of logic, yet experiments suggest there is more to it than that. The problem, called the Wason selection task, was devised by psychologist Peter Wason in 1966 and one version of it goes like this:

❓ PUZZLE 105A

You are presented with four cards lying on a table in front of you and you are told they each have a letter on one side and a number on the other. The faces you can see are as follows:

A   D   3   8

It is suggested that every card with a vowel on one side has an odd number on the other. The question is: which cards must you turn over to determine whether that statement is true?

Now here's another version of the problem:

❓ PUZZLE 105B

You are presented with four cards indicating destinations and modes of transport. You are told that every card has a destination name on one side and the word 'Bus' or 'Train' on the other. The faces you can see read as follows:

Leeds   Manchester   Bus   Train

Which cards must you turn over to determine whether the following statement is true:

'If you want to go to Leeds, you have to go by bus.'

As usual, you will find the answers and a discussion at the end of this book. Remarkably few of the people given puzzle 105a in Wason's original study gave the right answer (less than 10 per cent), but a matched group did much better at puzzle 105b, even though it demands exactly the same logical process.

One possible explanation is that people are more likely to solve problems that are presented in a socially relevant context rather than abstract formulations, but why so many people get the original Wason selection task wrong is still a bit of a mystery.

More recently, there has been much academic interest in the question of whether solving puzzles might actually be more than just a way of filling in the time while stuck on a train. Is it possible that puzzles are actually good for you?

Since the early 1980s, a theory that has become known as 'use it or lose it' has gathered support among psychologists. The phrase had previously been used in both physiological and legal domains, referring either to the benefits of exercise in maintaining the proper functioning of body parts or the legal right to claim exclusive use of trademarks, but it became increasingly used in discussing 'brain plasticity', referring to the importance of practising mental skills in order to develop or retain them. Specifically, the possible benefits of puzzles began to be advocated as a means of preventing, or at least delaying, mental degeneration.

In an article in *Psychology Today* in 2009, Marcel Danesi, Professor of Semiotics and Linguistic Anthropology at the University of Toronto, recalled work he had done with brain-damaged children in the mid-1980s in which he prepared puzzle material, such as jumbled letters, to improve the writing and reading skills of children who had been assessed as having a weak visual symbol memory. 'From that experience,' he wrote, 'it is my cautious opinion that puzzles are beneficial to brain activity.' While accepting that studies in this respect have produced ambiguous or inconclusive results, he goes on to say: 'There is little doubt in my mind that puzzles are beneficial ... I saw this with my own eyes within my own family. I once suggested to an ailing relative, who suffered from a serious brain-degenerative disease, to engage in crosswords and sudoku. He had never done puzzles in his life. His doctor immediately saw a significant slowing down of the degeneration.'

More recently, a team at Cambridge University, led by Professor of Clinical Neuropsychology Barbara Sahakian, has joined forces with a games developer to develop and test puzzle-like games designed to help reduce cognitive impairment. Specifically, they have studied the effects of a brain-training application called Game Show on the episodic memory of subjects diagnosed with schizophrenia. This is the part of memory that deals with questions such as 'Where did I leave my keys?' or 'Where did I park my car?', a decline in which may affect us all, but which has been found to deteriorate particularly in schizophrenics.

Designed to be fun to play to maintain the subjects' levels of interest, the game involves shapes appearing on a computer screen and flying into red boxes. It starts with 3 patterns flying into 6 boxes, and increases in difficulty to reach to up to 30 patterns and 30 boxes.

Remarkably, the study showed that 4 weeks after completing 8 hours of training on Game Show, subjects' performance on a standard test of episodic memory improved by as much as 40 per cent. Even more impressively, the game-playing produced results in many cases where supposedly brain-enhancing drugs had failed. As Professor Sahakian says, 'You should be stimulating your brain through the whole lifespan. We tend to do that early on as you're going to school and learning new things all the time, but later in life ... maybe you're not driving your brain to learn new things.'

Of course, to conclude, from a remedial study on schizophrenics involving a specially designed game, that puzzles in general are good for us would involve a huge leap, but later research published in 2017 confirmed the benefits of playing such games to a more general sample of people suffering mild cognitive impairment. The experiences and reach of such academics as Danesi and Sahakian go a long way to support the view that puzzles may be good exercise for our brains. Use it or lose it.

A vital ingredient in the success of the game mentioned above was that it should be fun and sustain interest, but the ingredients to provide this are elusive. Many games and types of puzzle have been invented over the ages, but only a few have survived the test of time and even fewer have created crazes. The first of these was, as mentioned earlier, Sam Loyd's 15-Puzzle, which gained a huge level of popularity in the closing years of the nineteenth century and had brief flurries of interest in later years. Then came crosswords, which are still a dominant force in the puzzle market, and it took half a century before another type of puzzle exerted a similar level of passion among puzzlers. This was the Rubik's Cube, which first appeared on the market in 1977 under the name 'Hungarian Magic Cube'.

The curious thing about this hugely successful invention is that Ernö Rubik was not a games inventor but an architect and a professor of agriculture. His original intention in designing the Rubik's Cube was as a way to get his students to think about three-dimensional objects through the ingenious invention of a hinge that allowed the interlocking pieces to be moved independently while holding the object firmly together. It was only when he tried to restore a previous pattern after scrambling it that he realized he had the basis of a successful puzzle toy.

After three years being made by a small Hungarian company, the Magic Cube was licensed worldwide and renamed 'Rubik's Cube'. One year later, three of the top ten bestselling books in the United States were instruction manuals for solving the Cube. By the end of 1982, over 200 million Cubes had been sold worldwide, but a year later the craze was over. Sales continued at a low level for almost 20 years, although interest has revived since 2000, partly because that was the year Rubik's patent expired and more companies began producing Cubes and entering the market.

So, what has been the secret behind the success of the Rubik's Cube, which – quite apart from general popularity – has led to intense competition for such records as the following (records as at the end of 2018)?

- 🏆 Fastest restoring of a Cube in an official competition: 4.22 seconds.
- 🏆 Fastest restoring using only one hand: 6.88 seconds.
- 🏆 Fastest restoring using only the feet: 20.57 seconds.
- 🏆 Fastest time to examine a cube, then restore it blindfolded: 17.33 seconds.

🏆 Most Cubes restored blindfold (after unlimited time examining them all): 48.

🏆 Most Cubes restored in 24 hours: 5,800.

Ernö Rubik himself later explained the fundamental lure of puzzles in general in words that applied well to his Cube: 'A good puzzle, it's a *fair thing*. Nobody is lying. It's very clear, and the problem depends just on you.'

As with crosswords, the Rubik's Cube offers a learning experience: the more you fiddle with it, the better you become, picking up the techniques required to get the colours where you want them, but – infuriatingly – that only applies up to a point. Most Cube users, after spending a great deal of time trying, found that they were able to restore one face or two faces to uniform colours, but attempts to go further led to frustration. Just as you think you are getting somewhere, you realize that you are messing up the sides you had previously completed. That frustration may explain why the craze died down in the mid-1980s.

As in many other areas of life, the first result of frustration is to stop trying, but the second is often to pick it up again later. Despite what the common proverb may advise, if at first you don't succeed, many people will be inclined to give up; but if the challenge is infuriating enough, they will try again at some later date.

The most recent puzzle craze to sweep the world has been that of sudoku. For seven years, these languished almost unknown in specialist puzzle books and magazines in the United States, where they were first seen in 1979 and called by the uninspiring name of 'number place'. Then, in 1986, they were introduced into Japan under the name 'sudoku', which was an abbreviation of a phrase meaning 'the digits must be single'.

In 1997, a judge in Hong Kong named Wayne Gould caught sight of sudoku puzzles in a Japanese magazine and then spent the next six years developing a computer program to generate them. In 2004, he sold the first sudoku to *The Times* newspaper in the UK, and other newspapers in both the UK and the USA quickly followed. Since then, there has hardly been a newspaper in either country that has not offered at least one daily sudoku puzzle.

Different-sized sudoku puzzles followed, as well as various grid-filling games such as killer sudoku and kakuro, but nothing has remotely matched the appeal of the original 9-by-9 sudoku.

Part of the attraction is the deceptive simplicity of the rules. The grid is divided into nine rows and nine columns, and contains nine 3-by-3 squares, each of which must contain just one of the digits from 1 to 9. A sudoku puzzle must have a unique solution to be considered valid.

Sometimes, they can be solved by simple logic,

sometimes by more complex deduction, and sometimes by a process involving, at some stage or other, an element of guesswork. Most papers now exclude any sudoku puzzles that require guesswork, which sudokuphiles refer to as 'outlaw'.

Since computers can solve any sudoku, whether it needs guesswork or not, in a fraction of a second, they have been used to assess a puzzle's difficulty level, based on the inherent difficulty, in human terms, of various techniques needed to complete them.

Mathematicians, needless to say, have taken an interest in sudokus, calculating, among other things, that there are 6,670,903,752,021,072,936,960 ways to fill in a completed solution grid. This reduces to 5,472,730,538, if we take into account various rotations, reflections and permutations of the numbers from 1 to 9. However, it is not known how many sudoku puzzles can be created that lead to identical final grids.

In 2012, three New York mathematicians completed an exhaustive computer search to demonstrate that any valid sudoku puzzle must have at least 16 digits in the initial set-up if it is to produce a unique solution.

As this is a puzzle book, I suppose I ought to include at least one sudoku, so here is perhaps the least wanted of all outlaws, created in 2012 by Finnish mathematician Arto Inkala, who claimed it was the world's hardest sudoku.

? PUZZLE 106

I definitely do not recommend you try this, but it may be worth giving it to any sudoku aficionado whom you wish to keep occupied for several hours.

8								
		3	6					
	7			9		2		
					7			
			4	5	7			
			1				3	
		1					6	8
		8	5				1	
	9					4		

In case you need any further putting off, I can reveal that the computer I used to solve this sudoku did so in a fraction of a second. It was equipped with all the logical techniques to complete sudokus but still needed to make 52 guesses, of which 23 led to dead ends.

In the wake of the success of sudoku, other computer-created puzzles with Japanese-sounding names such as kakuro, kenken, akari and takuzu began to appear on the market, but these generally had a larger arithmetical component than sudoku, which is based purely on logic and patterns. None of these has established itself in the way that sudoku has managed. But perhaps there is only room for one such puzzle in our culture.

We leave a final word on the psychological benefit of puzzles to Lewis Carroll, from the foreword of his book, *Symbolic Logic*:

> Mental recreation is a thing that we all of us need for our mental health; and you may get much healthy enjoyment, no doubt, from Games, such as Back-gammon, Chess, and the new Game 'Halma'. But, after all, when you have made yourself a first-rate player at any one of these Games, you have nothing real to *show* for it, as a *result!* You enjoyed the Game, and the victory, no doubt, *at the time*: but you have no *result* that you can treasure up and get real *good* out of. And, all the while, you have been leaving unexplored a perfect *mine* of wealth. Once master the machinery of Symbolic Logic, and you have a mental occupation always at hand, of absorbing interest, and one that will be of real *use* to you in *any* subject you may take

up. It will give you clearness of thought – the ability to *see your way* through a puzzle – the habit of arranging your ideas in an orderly and get-at-able form – and, more valuable than all, the power to detect *fallacies*, and to tear to pieces the flimsy illogical arguments, which you will so continually encounter in books, in newspapers, in speeches, and even in sermons, and which so easily delude those who have never taken the trouble to master this fascinating Art. *Try it.* That is all I ask of you!

'There is no darkness but
ignorance; in which thou
art more puzzled than the
Egyptians in their fog.'

Shakespeare, *Twelfth Night*

MISCELLANEOUS AND MYSTERIOUS

LET US RETURN to the question that we touched on in the previous chapter concerning the difference between puzzles and intelligence test items. A solver's approach to these is very similar: we build up a library of techniques for solving them and much of the battle is detecting which technique is appropriate to the question under consideration.

Anyone compiling items for an IQ test, however, is expected to stick to the rules, using only techniques which the solver may reasonably be expected to have encountered before. The puzzle-setter, however, feels free to invent new methods or combine old ones in a novel manner by way of disguise.

Try Puzzle 107, for example.

? PUZZLE 107

What is the next letter in the following series?

a, e, f, h, i, k, l, m, n ...

Hint: a natural transformation may help turn this question into one that you recognize or at least find easier to solve.

Now try this one.

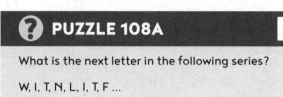

PUZZLE 108A

What is the next letter in the following series?

W, I, T, N, L, I, T, F ...

If you have seen that one before, ask yourself whether you would have been able to solve Puzzle 108b.

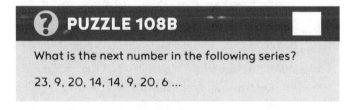

PUZZLE 108B

What is the next number in the following series?

23, 9, 20, 14, 14, 9, 20, 6 ...

And while we are on the subject, here's another one designed to confuse.

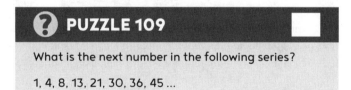

PUZZLE 109

What is the next number in the following series?

1, 4, 8, 13, 21, 30, 36, 45 ...

After such deliberately confusing items, you deserve a few easier ones, so here are some puzzles involving both letters and numbers, but with no misleading content about which is which:

? PUZZLE 110

The number ONE, when spelt out, has its letters in the reverse order in which they appear in the alphabet. It is the only number with that property, but which is the only number that has its letters, when spelt out, in alphabetical order?

Here are two more numerical spelling tests.

? PUZZLE 111A

I have 26 cards containing the letters of the alphabet, just one card for each letter. What is the largest number I can spell out without repeating any letter?

? PUZZLE 111B

Using the same 26 cards, what sum ? + ? = ? can I spell out?

I recently created some puzzles for the annual dinner of the chess-players at a London club. Knowing how much chess-players enjoy tackling unusual puzzles, I began by presenting them with the letters A, B, C, D, E, F and asking them which letter was the odd one out. After a short time, someone gave the right answer: it is D as all the others are initial letters of the surnames of world chess champions (Alekhine, Botvinnik, Capablanca, Euwe, Fischer). That, of course, could not be included in an IQ test as it is not culture fair but it has considerable bias towards chess-player puzzle-solvers.

Then I posed them a question that is definitely one of my favourites. It demands no chess knowledge and would, by most logicians at any rate, be considered fair:

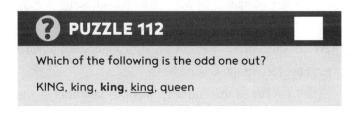

❓ PUZZLE 112

Which of the following is the odd one out?

KING, king, **king**, <u>king</u>, queen

Talking of odd ones out, I have always been a little suspicious of such puzzles as a bit of ingenuity is often enough to find a reason for anything in a list to be the odd one out (and that observation is a strong hint for the previous question), but see if you can get the same answer as I do to Puzzle 113.

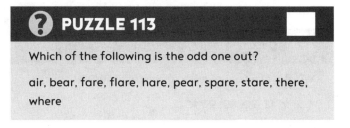

❓ PUZZLE 113

Which of the following is the odd one out?

air, bear, fare, flare, hare, pear, spare, stare, there, where

You may think it is 'air' because it is the only one without a letter 'e', or 'pear', as it is the only one a vegetarian can eat, or 'hare' as the only animal, but I think my answer is better.

As a further example of how a dastardly puzzle-setter's mind might work, let me give an example from many years ago when I was asked to provide a puzzle that was really, really difficult. This happened in Cambridge when I was in the company of some mathematician friends who were about to head to a problem-solving contest against their counterparts in Oxford.

They explained that, after the serious business of the independently set problems was over, they would have a little informal session when the two teams would set questions for each other. Could I, they wondered, suggest a puzzle that would flummox their opponents?

I saw this as an opportunity to test my idea of combining two very different ideas to generate something new and fair, but very difficult. Here is the puzzle I came up with, which did the job required perfectly.

❓ PUZZLE 114

What is the next number in the following series?

1, 2, 9, 12, 70, 89, 97, 102 ...

(I originally gave this series starting 2, 9, 12 ... but I just realized that a 1 can be added at the beginning. You may find it slightly easier without the '1', as you could help yourself a little by asking what sort of series begins with a 2.)

Here are another couple of examples of making things more difficult by adding a little something.

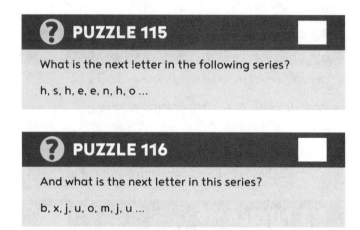

PUZZLE 115

What is the next letter in the following series?

h, s, h, e, e, n, h, o ...

PUZZLE 116

And what is the next letter in this series?

b, x, j, u, o, m, j, u ...

As at least one of the above puzzles shows, it is not always clear from the formulation of a question whether it is about numbers or letters, but as any good cryptographer knows, there is more than one way to disguise a letter or number. Try this one, which is very different from any of the preceding questions.

❓ PUZZLE 117

What comes next in this series?

2.1, 3.5, 3.3, 2.3, 1.3, 2.4, 2.5, 2.6, 1.8 …

Changing subject again, here is another question that demands a bit of common knowledge that has not yet been touched upon.

❓ PUZZLE 118

Which of the following words is the odd one out?

hasten, pairs, solo, iciest, animal, louse

And Puzzle 119 is a question with a historical appearance that actually has very little to do with history at all.

❓ PUZZLE 119

Which British King or Queen might be suitable to round off the following series?

Mary I, George III, Henry III, James II, George IV, Charles I …

And that concludes the main business of this book, but there is one more puzzle to come. The current chapter has explained some of the tricks that may be used to increase the perplexity of a puzzle. This should serve as an introduction to my final prize puzzle. The answer is hidden within the pages of this book. Indeed, it cannot be found without the help of this book. Have fun with it and don't be too disappointed if the answer does not leap out at you. The solution demands no special knowledge or abilities but, apart from that, I have made it as obscure as I can without being unfair.

THE PRIZE PUZZLE

? CLUE:

To reach your end, you'll need the ends,

Begin at the last and work back.

Add one each time, repeat these trends,

And you'll soon find the knack.

But remember, no matter how hard you look,

You won't find the answer without this book.

? THE PUZZLE:

What letter completes this sequence?

r, o, m, i, f, a, h, q, x ...

If you think you have the solution, send your answer, consisting of a single letter, together with your name, address and email, if possible, to:

William Hartston Prize Puzzle
Atlantic Books
Ormond House
26–27 Boswell Street
London
WC1N 3JZ

The competition will remain open until 1 December 2020, when entries will be opened in random order and a prize of £500 will be awarded to the first correct answer found.

The solution will be revealed on the Atlantic Books website.

Terms and Conditions

1. These terms and conditions apply to the competition entitled William Hartston Prize Puzzle.
2. Only one entry may be submitted per person. Senders of multiple entries will be disqualified.
3. The 'Entrant' is the person sending in their answer to the puzzle.
4. Entrants must be aged 18 or over. Entrants must be residents of Great Britain and must provide a valid British address upon entry. This competition is not open to employees or contractors of the Promoter, their immediate families, nor to any other person connected with the competition.

5. There will be 1 prize winner, who will win £500.

6. The Promoter reserves the right to amend the specification of the prize or offer an alternative prize of equivalent status. The prize is non-transferable.

7. Unsuccessful entrants will not be contacted. The decision of the Promoter on all matters is final.

8. A random draw of all valid entries will take place within six working days after the closing date above to select the winner. The winner will be notified by post or email, and MUST respond by midnight within seven days of the date of contact, providing a valid GB address for the prize to be dispatched to. If a selected winner does not meet all of the entry conditions or refuses the prize, another entrant will be selected at random from the remaining eligible entries within a reasonable timeframe.

9. The Promoter may terminate, amend or withdraw this draw and/or these terms and conditions at any time.

10. Entry to the competition is conditional on acceptance of these terms and conditions, which are governed exclusively by English Law and under the exclusive jurisdiction of the English courts. By entering this competition you are deemed to have read and accepted these terms.

11. The contact details you provide upon entry to the competition will be used by the Promoter to contact entrants if necessary to notify winners or to check eligibility requirements have been met, and will not be shared with other companies except to the extent necessary to provide the prize. The Promoter will only use your email address and other personal information in compliance with the provisions of the General Data Protection Regulation (including any amended, equivalent or subsequent legislation).

Promoter: Atlantic Books (company number: 04038606) whose registered office address is at Ormond House, 26-27 Boswell Street, London, WC1N 3JZ, UK.

SOLUTIONS

1 The first-year children were given two puzzles, then the numbers went up by 11 at a time, giving 13, 24, 35 and 46 to years 2, 3, 4 and 5 respectively. Easy to solve with a little algebra, but it must have been much more laborious for the ancient Egyptians.

2 Using P for a parent and C for a child, the river crossings are as follows:

C + C cross; one C returns.

P crosses; the other C returns.

C + C cross; one C returns.

P crosses; the other C returns.

C + C cross and the whole family are reunited on the other side of the river. Note how the children do most of the rowing.

3 First, take the goat across leaving the wolf with the cabbages. Return, then take the wolf across; on arrival, leave the wolf and grab the goat before the wolf can eat it and take it back again. On arriving back on the first side, unload the goat and leave it behind, put the cabbages in the boat and take them across. Finally, return, leaving the wolf and the cabbages together, and bring the goat over to join them.

4 If the boy's age is y years, twice his age is $2y$. Three times that age is $6y$. Adding one gives $6y + 1 = 100$. This means $6y = 99$, so $y = 16$ years 6 months.

5 It takes 17 crossings as follows (the man, woman, two boys, two girls, policeman and crook represented by M, W, B1, B2, G1, G2, P, C):

P + C; P returns.

P + B1; P + C return.

M + B2; M returns.

M + W; W returns.

P + C; M returns.

M + W; W returns.

W + G1; P + C return.

P + G2; P returns.

P + C.

6 This is the problem that gave rise to the famous Fibonacci sequence: 1, 1, 2, 3, 5, 8, 13, 21, 34, 55, 89, 144 … in which each number is equal to the sum of the two numbers preceding it. In any month, the number of rabbit pairs is equal to the number in the previous month (as they never die) plus the number in the month before that (which is equal to the number of newborn rabbit pairs born that month because each pair gives birth to one new pair after two months). In other words, the number of rabbit pairs is given by the Fibonacci sequence. Assuming the original rabbits are babies at the beginning, there will still be one pair after one month, two pairs after the second month and so on, according to the numbers given above. After 12 months, there will be 233 pairs of rabbits.

7 The fountain is 32 feet from the base of the lower tower and 18 feet from the base of the taller one. The answer comes from an application of Pythagoras' theorem. Drawing lines from the top of each tower to the fountain's position creates two right-angled triangles: the towers are their vertical lines, the lines from their bases to the fountain are their horizontals, and the birds' paths form the hypotenuses, which must be equal as the birds fly at the same speed and reach the fountain at the same time. Where x is the distance of the fountain from the foot of the lower tower, and h is the distance flown by the birds, applying Pythagoras to the lengths of the sides of these triangles then gives:

$$30^2 + x^2 = h^2 = 40^2 + (50 - x)^2$$

This gives $900 + x^2 = 1600 + 2500 - 100x + x^2$, which simplifies to $100x = 3200$, therefore $x = 32$.

8 The merchant started with 10½ denarii. You can work this out either forwards or backwards. If his money at the start is M, it progresses through 2M, 2M-12, 4M-24, 4M-36, 8M-72 and finally 8M-84, which we are told is zero so M must equal 10.5. Backwards is just as simple, when he must have had 12 denarii before spending it at the end, which would have been six before he doubled it, and 18 before he spent 12, and 9 before he doubled it, and so on, again reaching an initial figure of 10½.

9 Again, it's simple with algebra. If the sums held by the first, second and third men are F, S and T, we are told that:

F + 23 = 2S

S + 23 = 3T

T + 23 = 4F

Substituting first for T from the last of these equations (T = 4F-23), then for S (S = 3T-23), we arrive at:

F + 23 = 24F - 184

which gives:

23F = 207.

So, F = 9, from which it quickly follows that S = 16, T = 13.

10 Four weights of 1, 3, 9 and 27 pounds can be used to calculate the weight of any whole number of pounds up to 40 pounds. In general, the most efficient way to allocate the various weights on a balance is to use powers of three and the proof of this is very attractive.

Suppose we have a set of weights that can balance an object weighing any number of pounds up to a total of N pounds. We can then raise that number to 3N+1 by adding a single weight of 2N+1 to the set. The values from 1 to N pounds can be obtained as before by balancing the object being weighed with the old weights; values from N+1 to 2N can be calculated by subtracting the values of N to 1 from the new 2N+1 weight; finally, values from 2N+1 to 3N can be obtained by adding the old values of 1 to N to the new 2N+1 weight.

In this way, a single weight of 1 pound (N) can be used

to calculate the weight of zero or one. Adding a 3-pound weight $(3 = 2x1 + 1)$ brings us up to four pounds with two weights. Then a 9-pound weight $(9 = 2x4 + 1)$ brings it up to 13 pounds, and a 27-pound weight $(27 = 2x13 + 1)$ takes us to a total of 40 pounds.

It is, of course, no coincidence that the values of the weights are exact powers of 3, which comes out of the same mathematics.

11 This type of puzzle is sometimes referred to as the Josephus Problem as its earliest known occurrence was in the writings of the second-century Roman chronicler Hegessipus, who referred to a similar fate befalling a group of 41, led by a man called Josephus Flavius, who as a group committed suicide rather than be captured by Roman soldiers. According to a majority agreement, they all stood in a circle and killed every third one until only two remained. Josephus and an ally were the only ones opposed to suicide and chose places in the circle to ensure that they were the last two remaining alive.

In Bachet's (or Tartaglia's) version, with Christians (C) and Turks (T), the optimal arrangement for the Christians is CCCCTTTTTCCTCCCTCTTCCTTTCTTCCT. There is even a mnemonic to remember the order: *From numbers' aid and art, never will fame depart.* Just ignore the consonants and follow the vowels where *a* stands for 1, *e* for 2, *i* for 3, *o* for 4, and *u* for 5. So the order is *o* (4) Christians, *u* (5) Turks, *e* (2) Christians and so on.

12 Just follow this procedure:

You start with the 5pt, 3pt, 8pt vessels respectively holding (0, 0, 8).

Fill the 5pt to give (5, 0, 3).

Fill the 3pt from the 5pt to give (2, 3, 3).

Empty the 3pt into the 8pt: (2, 0, 6).

Pour the contents of the 5pt into the 3pt: (0, 2, 6).

Fill the 5pt from the 8pt: (5, 2, 1).

Fill the 3pt from the 5pt: (4, 3, 1).

Pour the 3pt into the 8pt: (4, 0, 4).

13 I find Newton's own explanation of how to answer this question hugely difficult to follow, but the following gets the same answer of 36 oxen, so his method was probably valid if incomprehensible.

There are three variables to take into account:

c = amount of grass chewed by one ox in a week;

a = amount of grass growing on one acre in one week;

i = initial amount of grass on one acre before the oxen start eating.

In 4 weeks, the amount of grass eaten by 12 oxen will be 12 x 4 x c, and as they graze $3\frac{1}{3}$ acres bare, this must equal $(10/3 \times 4 \times a) + 10/3 \times i$.

So: $48c = (40/3)a + (10/3)i$

Similarly, the other grazing statistics give us:

$(21 \times 9)c = (10 \times 9)a + 10i$

From these two equations, we may eliminate either i or c to get:

$c = (10/9)a$

and $i = 12a$.

If x oxen graze bare 24 acres in 18 weeks, then $x.18.c = 24.18.a + 24i$

Replacing c and i with the values obtained above, we get:
$x.(18.10)a/9 = 24.18a + 24.12a$

This gives: $20x = 24(18+12)$ which gives $x = 36$, and that's the number of Newton's oxen.

14 As you may have guessed, Carroll tells us that there was only one guest – but he did envisage rather a lot of intermarriage to allow it. He draws up the Governor's family tree (see below) back to one set of grandparents, who had two sons, whom we shall call Bertie (B) and Charles (C), and one daughter, Diana (d). Diana marries David (D) and they also have two boys, Edgar (E) and Frederick (F), as well as a daughter Gill (g). Edgar becomes Governor and marries the daughter of Bertie; Frederick marries the daughter of Charles; Gill marries the son of Charles; and all this makes Charles the proud bearer of all the relationships to the Governor (Edgar) specified in the question.

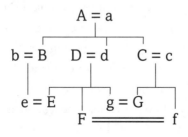

15 For every 100 men, we have 70 + 75 + 80 + 85 missing parts, which adds up to 310. The way to distribute these in order to give the lowest possible number of people missing all four parts, we would first assign three injuries to everyone, which leaves ten remaining injuries to assign to ten unfortunates. That gives only 10 per cent with all four parts missing.

16 ARMY – ARMS – AIMS – DIMS – DIME – DAME – NAME – NAVE – NAVY.

17 PIG – BIG – BAG – BAY – SAY – STY.

18 FLOUR – FLOOR – FLOOD – BLOOD – BROOD – BROAD – BREAD.

19 TRUMP – TRAMP – TRAMS – TEAMS – TERMS – TERES – CERES – CETES – CUTES – CUTIS – CUTIE – CUTIN – PUTIN.

20 Just imagine the column wrapped in a sheet of paper (with the garland on top). Make a cut in the paper from top to bottom and unwrap it. The garland will then appear as five straight diagonals, each from one side of the paper to the other, each on a right-angled triangle with a base of 16ft 8in and a height of 40ft. A simple application of Pythagoras' theorem then gives the length of each diagonal as 43ft 4in, so the total length of the garland is five times that, which is 216ft 8in. As Dudeney points out, 'A curious feature of the puzzle is the fact that with the dimensions given the result is exactly the sum of the height and the circumference.'

21 This is tricky as there are several routes the spider could take. 'Imagine the room to be a cardboard box,' Dudeney explains. 'Then the box may be cut in various different ways, so that the cardboard may be laid flat on the table.' In each case, the length of the spider's route may be calculated, as usual, by Pythagoras' theorem. The surprising thing is that the shortest route involves the spider walking across five of the six sides of the room: end wall, ceiling, side wall, floor, other end wall. That works out at 40ft compared with the more obvious route of end wall, floor, other end wall, which is 42ft.

22 The surprising answer is that one train must have been going twice as fast as the other. Suppose the speeds of the trains are v (the fast train) and w (the slower train) and when they meet, at time T, the fast train has travelled a distance a and the slower train a distance b. Then, $a = vT$ and $b = wT$, but also $a = 4w$ (as the slow train takes 4 hours to reach its destination) and $b = v$ (i.e. $1v$, as the fast train takes only 1 hour). So, $vT = 4w$ and $wT = v$. The first of these equations gives $T = 4w/v$, the second gives $T = v/w$, so we get $v/w = 4w/v$, which gives $v^2 = 4w^2$ so $v = 2w$.

In true British spirit, Dudeney says: 'I put this little question to a stationmaster, and his correct answer was so prompt that I am convinced there is no necessity to seek talented railway officials in America or elsewhere.'

23 There are two remarkable parts to this answer: the first is that a new century can never begin on a Sunday, the second is that this is true whether one considers that a new century begins with a year ending in -00, or one takes the strict view that the first century was from 1–100, so centuries begin in the -01 years. Dudeney's answer to the question, in which he stated that centuries do not begin on a Sunday, Tuesday or Thursday, makes it clear that he took the latter view.

The reason for all this is a quirk of the Gregorian calendar. Since 1582 in Catholic Europe and 1752 in England and most Protestant countries, we have adopted the calendar of Pope Gregory XIII, which has leap years every fourth year, except the hundreds, though every fourth hundred is again a leap year. So, 1800 and 1900 were not leap years, but 2000 was. That gives us 97 extra days every 400 years making a total of (400 x 365) + 97, which equals 146,097 days. That number is divisible by seven, so any 400-year period consists of a whole number of weeks and therefore returns to the same day of the week. So, 1 January 2200 will fall on the same day of the week as 1 January 1800, and 1 January 2201 will be the same day as 1 January 1801.

The days of the week of 1 January in 1801, 1901, 2001 and 2101 are Thursday, Tuesday, Monday, Saturday and those days will repeat for as long as we use the Gregorian calendar. Equally, 1 January in 1800, 1900, 2000 and 2100 falls on Wednesday, Monday, Saturday, Friday, so Sunday is avoided in either case.

24 1.Rh8+ Kxh8   2.Af5+ (remember that Alfils can jump) Kg8   3.Rh8+ Kxh8   4.g7+ Kg8   5.Nh6 mate. Note that 1.Nh6+ Kh8   2.g7+ Kh7   3.Af5 is not mate as Black can play 3...Kg6 where he is not in check from the Alfil.

25 Loyd did it in just 10 moves: 1.e3 a5   2.Qh5 Ra6 3.Qxa5 h5   4.h4 Rah6   5.Qxc7 f7   6.Qxd7+ Kf7   7.Qxb7 Qd3   8.Qxb8 Qh7   9.Qxc8 Kg6   10.Qe6 stalemate. A glorious creation.

26 1.d4 e5   2.Qd2 e4   3.a4 a5   4.Qf4 f5   5.h3 Qh4 6.Qh2 Bb4+   7.Nd2 d6   8.Ra3 Be6   9.Rg3 Bb3   10.c4 c5   11.f3 f4   12.d5 e3 stalemate.

27 1.b4 (obvious mating attempts with Rd5 or Rf5, intending Rd1 or Rf1 mate, would be met by 1... Rc5) Rc5 (the best defence)   2.bxc5 a2 (to stop Rb1 mate)   3.c6! Bc7 (3...bxc6 is met by 4.Rf5 and mate on f1 next move, but now 4.Rf5 is met by Bf4 putting off the mate by one move)   4. cxb7! and nothing can stop bxa8=B (or queen) mate next move. A great trip for the humble white b-pawn.

28 It takes 17 trips as follows, with ABCD representing the men and abcd their fiancées. The three items at each stage are the people on the starting shore, on the island, and on the other side.

Start: ABCDabcd – zero – zero
Trip 1: ABCDcd – zero – ab
Trip 2: ABCDbcd – zero – a

Trip 3: ABCDd – bc – a

Trip 4: ABCDcd – b – a

Trip 5: CDcd – b – ABa

Trip 6: BCDcd – b – Aa

Trip 7: BCD – bcd – Aa

Trip 8: BCDd – bc – Aa

Trip 9: Dd – bc – ABCa

Trip 10: Dd – abc – ABC

Trip 11: Dd – b – ABCac

Trip 12: BDd – b – ACac

Trip 13: d – b – ABCDac

Trip 14: d – bc – ABCDa

Trip 15: d – zero – ABCDabc

Trip 16: cd – zero – ABCDab

Trip 17: zero – zero – ABCDabcd

29 The way to solve this is backwards:

First, '… when Mary was three times as old as Ann' tells us that, at some time in the past, Ann's age was A when Mary's was 3A, so the difference in their ages, which remains constant, is 2A.

Then, 'when Ann is three times as old as Mary was …' clearly refers to a time when Ann's age will be 3 x 3A = 9A.

Mary is 'half as old' at that point, so she is 4.5A.

As the difference between their ages is 2A, Ann will then be 2.5A at the point when Mary is 4.5A.

We are told that Mary is now twice as old as that, which is 5A, so their ages are now 5A for Mary and 3A for Ann. As their ages add up to 44, so 8A = 44, from which we get that

$A = 5.5$.

So, Mary is now 27.5 and Ann is 16.5.

30 Across, in order of the clues: SALES, RECEIPT, MERE, DOVE, MORE, HARD, LION, EVENING, EVADE, ARE, FARM, RAIL, DRAW, TIED, SAND.

Down: DOH, MORAL, REVERIE, SERE, DOVE, FACE, NEVA, RULE, NARD, NEIF, SIDE, SPAR, TANE, TRADING, MIRED, LAD.

31 OXO (0 times 0 = nothing squared; oxo is a cube)

32 ITALIAN VERMOUTH (Gin and It)

33 ROVERS RETURN (The 'bar' [public house] in TV soap *Coronation Street*)

34 WATER (letters of alphabet from H to O; H_2O is water)

35 MIXED HERBS (letters of 'herbs' mixed up)

36 SCRAMBLED EGGS (letters of 'eggs' scrambled up)

37 DOUBLE AGENT (007 is a secret agent; double it to 014)

38 MANX CAT (the clue is 'cat' without its tail)

39 CIRCULAR LETTER (description of letter O)

40 HAS NOT GOT A CLUE (the same absent clue has been used for 'MISSING' or 'CLUELESS').

41 – 52 presbyterians, narcoleptic, retrogradely, waterfalls, holstering, solemnity, Germany, costumier, orchestral, interviews, totaliser, coarsest or coasters.

53 They are all anagrams of numbers: sine, ride, chess, chat are eins, drei, sechs, acht (1, 3, 6, 8 in German); riots, pest, zone are trois, sept, onze (3, 7, 11 in French). English has eon, tow, there, evens, net, tiffy and handouts (1, 2, 3, 7, 10, 50, thousand).

54 A carpet.

55 The answer is 'yes': 'one word' is an anagram of 'new door'.

56 'Pigeon' is an anagram of 'one pig'.

57 The words referred to are trifle, rifle, elf.

58 Pill, age, pillage.

59 Monosyllable.

60 Lace (L is Roman numeral for 50; ace is one in a pack of cards).

61 NICHE-IDLER-CLARA-HERDS-ERASE.

62 0 Love in Tennis

63 1 Day in the Life of Alexander Denisovich

64 2 Bottles of Champagne in a Magnum

65 3 Bears in Goldilocks

66 4 Leaves on a Lucky Clover

67 5 Toes on a Foot

68 6 Half a Dozen

69 7 Edges in a Heptagon

70 8 Equals Two Cubed

71 9 Lives of a Cat

72 10 Downing Street (not Deadly Sins which is 7 D S)

73 29 Letters in Floccinaucinihilipilification

74 Let's express what we know with the letters A, B, C, D, M representing both the crimes and the criminals. We write $X \to Y$ to mean that Mr X is accused of crime Y, so $X \to Y \to Z$

means Mr X is accused of Y and Mr Y is accused of Z. Then we know that C → ? → ? → M and M → ? → ? → A. Putting those together, we get C → ? → ? → M → ? → ? → A and all we have to do is work out where B and D fit in.

Since each person is charged with only one crime and each crime is associated with only one criminal, the letters must go round in circles. The cycles forming these circles cannot be of length one, as no-one is charged with the crime bearing his own name. So there cannot be a cycle of four, as that would leave one person out who would have to be charged with his own crime. Given the distance between C, M and A in our cycle, these cannot be a cycle of three, so the only possibility is that we have one cycle with five elements, so C must recur five steps away from the start of our cycle which now becomes C → ? → ? → M → ? → C → A, which also puts A into the second position after C.

We are left with just two possibilities: C → A → D → M → B → C or C → A → B → M → D → C. The first of these is ruled out as we know that D received a jail term so he could not be the murderer, so the murderer must be Mr Battery.

75 C has a black hat. If he had a white hat, then A's response would rule out the possibility that B also had a white hat, as A would then have seen two white hats and therefore have known that his own must be black. Seeing C's white hat would then have told B that his hat must be black, so he would have said 'Yes'. When he answers 'No', C knows his hat is black.

76 What happens is nothing for the first 49 times the lights are turned on, then on the 50th trial, all the logicians say they are wearing white hats. Consider what would happen if there were only two logicians. When the lights first go on, they both see the other is wearing a white hat. They do not know the colour of their own hat, but realize that if it is black, the other logician will immediately recognize that his own hat must be white as they are told that at least one has a white hat.

With three logicians, they all see two white hats at first, so know that if their own hat is black, the owner of the white hat is reduced to only two for the other logicians, which reduces the problem to the case of two logicians – which, as we have already seen, takes only two flashes of the lights. So, when nobody identifies their colour on the third trial, they all know their hats must all be white. The number of times the lights are turned on goes up by one each time the number of logicians is raised by one.

77 The structure is exactly the same as in the previous puzzle. If there were only two couples, each wife would see the other's adulterous spouse while thinking their own faithful. When they see the other husband still there a week later, they realize the other wife must have known their own husband was an adulterer. After 50 weeks, they all simultaneously kick their husbands out.

78 In general, if the numbers on the hats are a, b and c, then the logic works like this. A can only know his number if b=c. If that is not the case, B will know his number if a=c or a=2c. In the latter case, B reasons that his number must be 3c or c, but it cannot be c, or A would have known his number. Similarly, C will know his number if a=b, or a=2b, or b=2a, or a and b are in the ratio 2:3, for in the last case he knows his number is not the difference between the other two, for that would mean that a=2c when B would have known his number. Going back to A, he will be able to tell his own number if a:b:c are in the ratio 8:3:5, for his number cannot then be the difference between the other two, or C would have known his number last time. When the question passes to B again, he can add 8:13:5 to the ratios that tell him his number, as his number cannot be the difference of the other two without A having been able to work out his own number.

So when B says '13', we know that A has 8 and C has 5. With any other numbers, B would not have been able to work out that his own number was 13.

79 Think about C's reasoning. It is clear that he did not see four blue or four yellow stamps, since he would then have known that he had two of the other colour. He also could not have seen two blues on one of A or B and two yellows on the other, for then he would have known that he had one blue and one yellow – otherwise, either A or B would have seen four stamps of the same colour and deduced his own colours. So, it is impossible for both A and B to have two stamps of the same colour, which means that at least one of them must have one blue and one yellow stamp. When it came to A's second turn,

A knew that if B had two stamps of the same colour, his own stamps must be different colours. When A said that he didn't know the colours of his own stamps, B deduced that he must be the one with a blue stamp and a yellow stamp.

80 The prisoners can save at least 99 of their number if they follow this simple strategy. The night before the executions, they agree that the first prisoner, who can see the 99 hats in front of him, will say 'Black' if he sees an odd number of black hats and 'White' if the number of black hats is even. The next man can then tell the colour of his own hat by counting the number of black hats in front of him and seeing if the quality of being odd or even has changed by his own hat being excluded. That tells him whether his own hat is black or white. Other prisoners listen to all the answers and adjust the parity as appropriate.

81 Again, the first prisoner can say 'Black' or 'White' to establish whether the number of black hats is odd or even (the parity). The next man then performs his own count, which will tell him whether he has a black hat. If he has, he says 'Black'; if he hasn't (i.e. the parity is the same as the first man's) he says 'Red' or 'White' to let everyone know the parity of the red hats. Each subsequent man can then tell if he has a black hat or a red hat, and if neither of those, it must be a white hat. Only one parity change is possible each time, so 98 of the prisoners will be saved. In general, if m different colours of hats are used, the prisoners can save $(101-m)$ of their number.

82 The white king must be on c3. Here's how it had to happen: add a white king on b3, white pawn on c2, and a black pawn on b4. Black has just moved his bishop to d5 giving check. White replies c4 and Black takes that pawn *en passant* delivering the apparently impossible double-check. White then plays Kxc3, which explains why the king has to be on c3.

83 Black's moves must have been 1.e5 (or e6), 2.Qf6, 3.Qxf3+ 4.Be7 mate.

84 If the first sign is true, then so is the second one, which we are told is not the case. So the second sign is true and the first is false. The second sign says that there is a lady in one room and a tiger in the other, and as we know the first sign is false, it has to be the tiger behind door A and the lady behind door B.

85 Both signs cannot be false: if the second sign is false, then Room A contains a lady, which makes the first sign true. So both signs must be true. Therefore, a tiger is in Room A and a lady in Room B, so again you should choose Room B.

86 If the second sign is false, there must be a tiger in Room A, which would make the Room A sign correct. So both signs cannot be false, so they must both be true. That means that there is a lady in Room A (by the sign on Room B) and there must be a lady in Room B as well (to make the second half of sign A correct).

87 The parrot is deaf.

88 Nine (four and five is nine – you cannot argue with that).

89 When the man says 'we are both knaves' he cannot be telling the truth because that's not what knaves do. So the man and his wife are not both knaves. But the man must be a knave (since he cannot be telling the truth) so his wife must be a knight (to make his statement false).

90 He's a knight and she's a knave. If what he says is false, then neither of them is a knave, which means both are knights which makes his statement true, which is a contradiction. So what he says is true and he is a knight, and his wife then has to be a knave.

91 Suppose he is a knight, then he tells the truth so his statement is true: if he is a knight, then so if his wife. So his wife must also be a knight. But he said, '*If* I am a knight, then so is my wife,' so we have proved that what he says is true: if he is a knight, so is his wife. Since it is true, he must be a knight – and so is his wife.

92 Let's call the guards True, Lie and Random. Number the guards 1, 2, 3 and ask Guard 1: 'Is one and only one of the following statements true: "You are True and Guard 2 is Random"?'

If the guard says 'Yes', there are three possibilities:

1. Guard 1 is True and Guard 2 is Lie.

2. Guard 1 is Lie and Guard 2 is True.

3. Guard 1 is Random.

If the guard says 'No' to the first question, there are again three possibilities:

1. Guard 1 is True and Guard 2 is Random.

2. Guard 1 is Lie and Guard 2 is Random.

3. Guard 1 is Random.

If the answer to the first question is 'Yes' we address our second question to Guard 2, and if it is 'No' we address it to Guard 3. In either case, however, we avoid Random, so we may safely ask: 'What would you say if I asked you which was the road to Heaven?'

93 Several learned philosophical papers have been written about this question but it all boils down to this:

Question one, as in the previous puzzle, involves identifying one of the men who is definitely not Random.

Question two determines whether the man we have identified is True or Lie.

Question three tells us the identities of the other two.

Here's the simplest set of questions:

First, pick the man in the middle and ask: 'If I asked you whether the man on your left is Random, would you say "ja"? If the man in the middle is Random, the answer is meaningless, but remarkably, if the man you are talking to is either True or Lie, it doesn't matter which of 'ja' and 'na' is 'yes' and which is 'no', or whether you are talking to True or Lie, if the answer is 'ja' the man on the left is Random, if it is 'na' the man on the right is Random.

So, if we get the answer 'ja' we address our second question to the man on the right and if we get the answer 'na' we choose the man on the left. That way, we are sure to avoid Random.

Having chosen who to ask, we now pose the question, 'If I asked whether you are Lie, would you say "ja"?' It doesn't matter whether 'ja' means 'yes' or 'no', if the answer is 'ja' the man we are talking to is Lie, and if it is 'na' he is True.

We then ask him, 'If I asked you whether the man in the centre is Random, would you say "ja"?' His answer will let us identify all three men – even though we still do not know which of 'ja' and 'na' is 'yes' and which is 'no'.

94 Start by weighing coins 1+2+3+4 against 5+6+7+8.

If they balance, then we know the fake coin must be 9, 10, 11 or 12. In this situation, weigh 9+10+11 against 1+2+3 (which we know are all good). If these balance, then we know 12 is the fake and only have to weigh 12 against 1 to see whether it is overweight or underweight. If 9+10+11 does not balance against 1+2+3, then we know one of those is the fake and we also know whether it is overweight or underweight, according to which side of the balance is heavier. We then weigh 9 against 10: if they balance, then 11 is the fake; if they do not balance then, as we know whether the fake is heavier or lighter, we know which one it is.

If the original weighing of 1+2+3+4 against 5+6+7+8 does not balance, then one side is heavier than the other. Let's suppose it is 1+2+3+4 that is heavier. We then weigh 1+2+5 against 3+4+6. If they balance, then one of 7 or

8 must be underweight. We can tell which by weighing 7 against 1.

The only case left is if 1+2+5 and 3+4+6 do not balance – let's suppose 1+2+5 is the heavier side. Then either 1 or 2 is overweight, or 6 is underweight. So our final weighing is 1 against 2. If they balance, 6 is the fake coin and is underweight; if they do not balance, the heavier one is the fake.

95 Weigh the weights labelled 1, 2, 3 against the weight labelled 6. If they do not balance, then we know an error has been made. If they do balance, then since this is the only way three weights can equal a single weight, we know that the weight labelled 6 is correct and those labelled 1, 2, 3 are the 1g, 2g, 3g, although not necessarily in the right order. So the only possible errors are either some permutation among 1, 2, 3, or the 4 and 5 being the wrong way round.

We then weigh 1+6 against 3+5. If they balance, then an error has clearly been made (which is all the question asks you to identify), as is also the case if 1+6 is heavier than 3+5. The only other possible outcome is when 3+5 is heavier than 1+6, which can only occur if all the weights are correctly labelled, as 3+5 weighs at most 8 and 1+6 is at least 7.

96 Using the same notation as in the solution to puzzle 12, the 4pt, 7pt, 9pt containers start off with (0, 0, 9), and the first steps are: (4, 0, 5), (0, 4, 5), (4, 4, 1), (1, 7, 1). You then empty the 7pt container into the barrel, leaving (1, 0, 1) and finish it off with (1, 1, 0).

97 This takes longer. Start with (0, 0, 22) in the 4pt, 7pt and 22pt containers. The first steps are (0, 7, 15) and (4, 3, 15), then empty the first container into the barrel and continue (0, 3, 15), (3, 0, 15), (3, 7, 8), (4, 6, 8), into the barrel (0, 6, 8), then (4, 2, 8), into the barrel (0, 2, 8), then (2, 0, 8), (2, 7, 1), (4, 5, 1), into the barrel (0, 5, 1), then (4, 1, 1), into the barrel for the last time (0, 1, 1), and finally (1, 1, 0).

98 Suppose the time the first cyclist spends resting is R and the time the second spends resting is S, then the times they spend cycling must be 2S and 3R respectively. So, the total times taken by the cyclists are (2S + R) and (S + 3R) respectively, but we are told these are the same, so by simple algebra S = 2R. The times they spent actually on their bikes are therefore equal to 4R (first rider) and 3R (second rider), so, as they covered the same distance, the second must have been the faster rider.

99 You can solve this by summing an infinite series of the fly's journey, but the simple way is to say that the relative speed of the trains is 50mph and they meet midway, which is 50 miles along the track, after 1 hour. The dragonfly's speed is 35mph so in that hour it will have covered 35 miles.

100 The only solution is: 53,086 + 53,086 = 106,172.

101 The only solution is: 109,368 + 109,368 + 109,368 = 328,104.

103 The only solution is: 413 x 418 = 172,634.

104 As the service is regular, the number of buses at any given moment on the route is constant. Let us call that number B. Going in an opposite direction to the buses, the driver will meet all those buses on the route when she starts (B), plus all those buses that start the journey in the hour she is driving. Let's call that extra number C. Then, B + C = 16. Going in the other direction, she will overtake all the buses on the route when she starts (B), minus the number that complete the journey before she can overtake them but while she is on the road. That latter number must be the same as the number of buses that start the journey in the same time (i.e. C), because the number on the road remains constant. So B - C = 8. This gives us B = 12 and C = 4, so 4 buses start their journey every hour, which means buses run every 15 minutes.

104 If the man's speed is m and the escalator's speed is e, his speed travelling down is $m + e$ and his speed travelling up is $m - e$. So, if d is the length of the escalator:

$d/(m + e) = 1$

and

$d/(m - e) = 3$

These give us:

$d = m + e$

and

$d = 3m - 3e$

Multiplying the first equation by three ($3d = 3m + 3e$) and subtracting the second equation, to eliminate m, gives $2d = 6e$. This means that $d = 3e$, so d/e, which is the time the escalator takes on its own, is equal to 3 minutes.

105a The cards that need to be turned over are A and 8. Either an even number on the other side of the A or a vowel on the other side of the 8 would disprove the assertion. The other two cards are irrelevant.

105b The cards you must turn over are Leeds and Train. This question is answered correctly by far more people than question 105a is, although the two are logically equivalent.

106

8	1	2	7	5	3	6	4	9
9	4	3	6	8	2	1	7	5
6	7	5	4	9	1	2	8	3
1	5	4	2	3	7	8	9	6
3	6	9	8	4	5	7	2	1
2	8	7	1	6	9	5	3	4
5	2	1	9	7	4	3	6	8
4	3	8	5	2	6	9	1	7
7	9	6	3	1	8	4	5	2

107 t (turn them into capitals, A, E, F, H, I etc., and you will see them as the letters made up of straight lines only, with no curves).

108a S (they are the first letters of the words in the question).

108b 19 (they are the alphabet positions of the first letters of the words in the question).

109 54 (each number in the series is obtained by adding the number of letters in the previous number to that number).

110 FORTY.

111a FIVE THOUSAND.

111b SIX + FOUR = TEN.

112 At first sight, queen looks the odd one out, as the others are all kings. But on second, third and fourth sight, KING is the only one in capitals, **king** is the only one in bold type, and <u>king</u> is the only one that is underlined, so king is the odd one out, because it is the only one that is not the odd one out!

113 The odd one out is *spare* as all the others are homophones of other words that sound the same: heir, bare, fair, flair, hair, pair, stair, their, wear.

114 Subtracting one from each number gives the series: 0, 1, 8, 11, 69, 88, 96, 101, which are the numbers that are not changed by turning them upside down. The next in that series is 111, so the answer is 112.

115 e (they are the second letters of the words in the question).

116 t (they are one letter further along in the alphabet than the opening letters of the words in the question).

117 The answer is 2.7. They are the positions on a standard typewriter keyboard of the letters of the alphabet in order: A is 2.1 (the first letter on the second row), B is 3.5, the fifth letter on the third row, and so on.

118 Iciest. The others are all anagrams of capital cities: Athens, Paris, Oslo, Manila, Seoul. Iciest, incidentally, is an anagram of 'cities'.

119 Henry I, Harold I or Charles II would all be correct. Mary I refers to the first letter of Mary (i.e. 'M'), George III is the third letter of George (i.e. 'o') and so on. The items spell out the letters MONARC and need an H to complete the series.

A NOTE ABOUT THE AUTHOR

William Hartston graduated in mathematics at Cambridge but never completed his PhD in number theory because he spent too much time playing chess. This did, however, lead to his winning the British Chess Championship in 1973 and 1975 and writing a number of chess books and newspaper chess columns.

When William and mathematics amicably separated, he worked for several years as an industrial psychologist specializing in the construction and interpretation of personality tests. After ten years writing a wide variety of columns for the *Independent*, he moved to the *Daily Express*, where he has been writing the Beachcomber column of surreal humour since 1998. In addition to writing about chess, he has written books on useless information, numbers, dates and bizarre academic research, including sexology.

Recently, his skills at sitting on a sofa watching television have been appreciated by viewers of the TV programme *Gogglebox*, but he has still not decided what he wants to be when he grows up.